NOTES TOWARD A
DIGITAL WORKERS'
INQUIRY

NOTES TOWARD A
DIGITAL WORKERS'
INQUIRY

The Capacitor Collective

Brooklyn, NY
Philadelphia, PA
commonnotions.org

ISBN: 978-1-945335-48-8 | eBook ISBN: 978-1-945335-60-0
Library of Congress Number: 2025943464

10 9 8 7 6 5 4 3 2 1

Common Notions
c/o Interference Archive
314 7th St.
Brooklyn, NY 11215

Common Notions
c/o Making Worlds Bookstore
210 S. 45th St.
Philadelphia, PA 19104

www.commonnotions.org
info@commonnotions.org

Discounted bulk quantities of our books are available for organizing, educational, or fundraising purposes. Please contact Common Notions at the address above for more information.

Cover design by Josh MacPhee
Layout design and typesetting by Sydney Rainer
Printed by union labor in Canada on acid-free paper

The Capacitor Collective's *Notes Toward a Digital Workers' Inquiry* is supported in part by funding from the Social Sciences and Humanities Research Council of Canada.

CONTENTS

PREFACE

A capacitor is a device that accumulates electric energy across two surfaces that are insulated from each other. By choosing this object as our collective name, we stress how research and labor organizing need not be separated: if circuits connecting them are built and activated, energy accumulates between the two poles and explosive things can happen. This book describes, theorizes, and circulates experiences of *digital workers' inquiry*, or collaborative research that feeds into labor organizing within and against digital capitalism.

Digital workers' inquiry aims to narrow the gap between organizing and research, combining them to the point that research becomes organizing and organizing becomes research. As Mostafa Henaway puts it, "the more distance you have from the ground and the activism, your analysis becomes more obscure, less rigorous and sharp. When you're grounded . . . it enriches both the research and the activism."[1] Rather than focusing on the technologies, algorithms, or managerial techniques that are used to dominate labor, a digital workers' inquiry starts from the experiences of workers and their inherent capacity for resistance and counter-organization. Digital workers' inquiry is not a research method, it is a political approach to the production of knowledge from below, beginning from our locations

1

within—and struggles against—digital capital. Like a capacitor, digital workers' inquiry makes possible strong reciprocal interactivity and builds power that can feed struggles.

The Capacitor Collective is a research group committed to digital workers' inquiry. The six members who edited this book—Enda Brophy, Julie Chen, Alessandro Delfanti, Brian Dolber, Lilly Irani, and Tamara Kneese—collectively authored the opening essay and epilogue, but imagining and writing this project has involved ongoing discussions and research with many individual workers, unions, and other worker-led organizations engaged in collective action along the digital value chain. Our collective's members are mostly based across the US and Canada, and as such, this book reflects organizations we have worked with directly: Alphabet Workers Union, Amazon Workers Solidarity, Collective Action in Tech, Gig Workers United, No Tech for Apartheid, Tech Workers Coalition, Pittsburgh Tech Workers United, Rideshare Drivers United, Turkopticon, United Taxi Workers of San Diego, and Vice Union. Our connections with these organizations range from full membership and collaborations where we actively contribute to research efforts in the context of political struggles, to knowledge exchanges with individual workers and organizers at dedicated events and more informal settings. The book does not represent these organizations' collective views, but it is informed by their organizing and the conversations and collaborations we have had with their members over the years. Several additional researchers—Hiu-Fung Chung, Catherine Dubé, Victoria Fleming, Seamus Bright Grayer, Diana Limbaga, Sarah Jean Salman, and Véronique Sioufi—contributed critical ideas and insights, conducted interviews, and assisted with the development of this project in other significant ways. The research for and publication of this book were supported in part by a grant from the Social Sciences and Humanities Research Council of Canada.

This book is the result of a collective effort that cuts across divisions between academia and the broader workforce in the digital economy. The book consists of two parts. The first is a collectively written essay, "Notes Toward a Digital Workers' Inquiry." Here, we situate digital workers' inquiry, outline its features, and argue for its importance in an economy where platforms, algorithms, and artificial intelligence are predominant. Our analysis is informed by years of discussion, alliance, and complicity with workers rebelling against digital capital, as well as the rich set of conversations that appear in the second part of the book. The second section gathers eleven interviews conducted between 2021 and 2024 with labor activists involved in organizing at e-commerce, software production, delivery and ride-hailing, and other tech companies. The interviews focus on the dynamic interplay between labor research and organizing and how scholars can foster solidarity with workers and their associations so as to build a more powerful labor movement. In the book's Epilogue, we reflect on the role of a digital workers' inquiry in a moment of political backlash and tech's alignment with authoritarian rule.

Based on our own geographic positioning, the book is heavily skewed toward North American experiences, organizations, and political cultures, but interviews from Scotland and China highlight how experiments in inquiry from below support labor organizing in different national environments and technological frameworks. Importantly, the stories of workers' inquiry that make up this book intersect communities with very different compositions in terms of class, gender, race, and status. What reconciles them are the alliances they sometimes form and their common goal of resisting new and old conditions of exploitation. We hope this text can act as a spark that recharges our collective capacity to produce knowledge in academia and beyond, and to organize across the fractures and barriers imposed on us by digital capitalism.

PART 1

NOTES TOWARD A DIGITAL WORKERS' INQUIRY

Enda Brophy, Julie Chen, Alessandro Delfanti, Brian Dolber, Lilly Irani, and Tamara Kneese

An upswing of labor resistance, unionization, and autonomous self-organization is happening at multiple points along
digital capitalism's value chains—from the workers building
the software to those whose precarious labor on the very
margins of the labor market is governed by algorithms. Since
the mid-2010s, this resurgence has been remarkable in its
scope and variety, from the uncoordinated, invisible, below-
the-surface movements of "quiet quitting" and its China-
based equivalent "*tang ping*" ["lying flat"], to struggles over
remote work and contracting out, to the actual organizing
campaigns, strikes, and walkouts by workers at tech contractors, e-commerce warehouses, and food delivery apps.[1] Yet,
by and large, researchers tend to represent these workers as
powerless, invisible, and subject to exploitation and oppres-
sion by forces they cannot control.

While bringing attention to the deeply uneven power
dynamics between labor and capital is important, knowledge production must consider workers' own perspectives,
desires, and concerns. Although the kinds of labor that digital
capitalism requires are often highly exploited and invisible,

5

workers are always already capable of self-organization,
even in the most challenging of circumstances. The truth is
that only knowledge from below—knowledge generated by
and for workers—can fully grasp labor's creativity, potential, and power.

As with any social movement, workers often use grassroots research as part of their organizing and mobilization.[2]
"Research is the lifeblood of our strategy," said one platform
worker in discussing how knowledge can be used to assume
an offensive posture instead of simply reacting to capital's
actions. For instance, e-commerce warehouse workers study
their companies to identify the chokepoints that could be
vulnerable to labor action and the best tactics to impact them.
Workers who tag or clean data for machine-learning training that makes "artificial intelligence" through crowd-work
platforms use research to understand the composition of the
workforce and its diversity in terms of demographics, geographic location, and economic treatment. App-based food
couriers do research to unveil how opaque algorithmic decisions determine task assignments and worker deactivation.
Rideshare drivers screenshot and share app requests in social
media forums or group chats so that they can study why and
how they may receive different fees for the same order, or as
they all decline fares during a strike (see our conversation with
Shenzhen V Fleet organizer Qi Ge, pp. 137). Microtask workers at Amazon Mechanical Turk (AMT) turn their collective
gaze toward "requesters," those who hire them for "human
intelligence tasks" (HITs), by using purpose-built software
that can identify those who engage in wage theft or treat
workers poorly (see our conversation with Turkopticon's
Krystal K and Phil, pp. 57). Some researcher-organizers have
called for what they refer to as algorithmic or *data workers'*
inquiry, a form of data collection and tool development that
gives platform workers recourse against algorithmic wage
discrimination, directly using data-based research to inform

their strategies.[3] The need to understand the global division of labor at a multinational corporation requires research, too; for instance, to organize across the divide between engineers and contracted-out data entry workers, cooks, or cleaners at tech companies, and thus build wall-to-wall solidarity regardless of education, specialization, and other markers of fragmentation (see conversations with Tech Workers Coalition organizers RK Upadhya and Erik H, pp. 89, 105).

We see all these different ways to produce knowledge from below as forms of *digital workers' inquiry*, a term which has increasingly been circulating in recent years.[4] We take it up to refer to a wide range of collaborative research and knowledge-sharing practices which can feed into labor organizing efforts within and against digital capitalism writ large. Digital workers' inquiry is a form of knowledge production that gathers, assists, and shapes forms of struggle from below. This approach to research can be formal or informal, systemic or ephemeral. It can be pursued with automated digital data collection methods, or through more traditional social science strategies such as interviews or ethnographies with the workers of digital capitalism. In any case, digital workers' inquiry draws on the situated experiences of workers and the relevant skills of researchers to expose, subvert, and overturn digital capitalism's technologically mediated power.

We are inspired by the militant tradition of workers' inquiry, especially the research conducted in the 1960s and '70s in Italy by sociologists and independent researchers within the tradition of *operaismo* [workerism], which studied the emergent Fordist industrial economy—ranging from factory work to domestic labor—in collaboration with workers and toward revolutionary goals.[5] Workers' inquiry adopts an irreducibly partisan position, as it is research that is not only always on the side of labor but always and explicitly anticapitalist. As a corollary of labor's primary role in capitalist development, workers' inquiry centers labor resistance, even those invisible forms of organization that are hidden or difficult to see on the surface.[6] As the methodological offshoot of radical, worker-led social movements, workers' inquiry openly challenges the division between the researcher and their "subject," instead encouraging collaboration whenever possible. If all is going as it should, the research supports the organizing and the organizing feeds into the research.

This remains true in digital capitalism, albeit the forms these inquiries take, the ways they are produced, and how they can be shared are substantially different from those typical of twentieth-century industrial capitalism. Digital platforms and technologies have contributed to restructuring the labor process, most notably through forms of algorithmic management that mediate the relationship between workers and employers. It is also crucial to understand the algorithmic reorganization of labor is based on capital's newly acquired ability to automate the generation of information on the labor process: the extraction and algorithmic crunching of digital data from workers' activities amounts to a new kind of knowledge production for capital. Increasingly, the data used to analyze and control labor reside on distant servers inaccessible to workers, are computed by billion-dollar proprietary technologies, and feed into all-too-human forms of workplace power that benefit from decades of labor restructuring and the defeat of labor organizations in many industries (see our conversation with Cailean Gallagher, Workers' Observatory, pp. 145).

Workers may seem powerless in the face of capital's new epistemic power, but as we argue here, a digital workers' inquiry can challenge and subvert this knowledge monopoly. A digital workers' inquiry is not simply the application of a set of research methods to a problem. As theorized by *operaismo*, struggles and conflicts not only impose new directions on capitalist development, but they also generate new kinds of knowledge from below—including new experiences, new

connections, and new organizational forms. Adapting Mario
Tronti's explosive insights,[7] we argue that in this transitory
situation, workers within digital capitalism appear to be
testing out (and sometimes moving beyond) older forms of
collective organization—without yet having settled on new
forms that can overturn the mode of production entirely
once again. Within this uncertainty, the starting point for
our research are the new forms of digital workers' struggle.
These have the potential not only to impose a different kind
of capitalist development, but to generate new kinds of subversive knowledge and organization. The urgent need for
knowledge about capital's goals, management's tools, and
counterstrategies to be used in organizing feeds this knowledge from below.

The analysis of class composition—the complex and
ever-changing makeup of the working class—is always at
the core of workers' inquiry. Traditionally, this has meant
the analysis of two complementary characteristics: technical
and political composition. Technical composition is the form
in which technological and managerial principles organize
labor on the shop floor and thus the social relations of work.
Political composition is the self-organization of workers to
confront capital: their political cultures, tactics of resistance,
and power-building. An in-depth understanding of both and
the relationship between them, workerists argued, is the necessary condition for organizing.

In recent years, that tradition has been rediscovered and
updated to better grasp the circuits of the digital economy. For
instance, the UK-based journal *Notes from Below* has added the
analysis of social composition—that is, the social relations that
shape the workforce beyond the workplace, including race,
gender, dis/ability, as well as consumption and reproduction
processes.[8] A digital workers' inquiry aims to support the leap
from technical and social to political composition, or what
operaismo called *recomposition*.[9] This is a political strategy,

sustained by attention to the social and political determinants of worker struggles and workers' knowledge of the conditions under which labor takes place. The aim is to unite an artificially divided working class and find ways to make its struggles more effective.

In the following sections, we present various concrete examples in three areas where a digital workers' inquiry can contribute to recomposition: (1) the generation of knowledge about the working class within digital capitalism; (2) the bottom-up analysis of the nature and application of digital technology on the shop floor; and (3), the tactical use of research to identify bottlenecks in production processes or other chokepoints where workers' power can be leveraged. First, we address the epistemic question behind a workers' inquiry approach to producing knowledge from below through labor research: *whose knowledge?*

STAKING OUR POSITION

As scholars based in the neoliberal university who study labor and digital technologies, over the last two decades we have witnessed a proliferation of scholarship on labor that is mediated, organized, and controlled by digital technology. While we are happy to see the efforts of many colleagues drawn to this critically important dimension of social life, we have serious questions about the ways some of this research has unfolded. Much of it appears to be ambivalent or even apolitical in its orientation, and extractive in its nature.

A paradigmatic example of this is when university-based scholars parachute into a labor community—these days, usually platform-based gig workers—in order to extract knowledge from workers. They then present their findings solely for academic audiences, in specialized journals behind paywalls or at conferences with exorbitant registration fees. Rarely do these researchers ever give back—or even go back—to the labor community from which that knowledge derives. While we consider the troubling dynamics of university-based research further below, more recently we've seen developments specific to the era of digital capitalism.

Above all, in this era, "Big Tech" plays a dominant role in knowledge production. Companies pour millions into think tanks that heavily influence the conversation around the role of digital technology in our societies. They hire researchers, seed research institutes and internal AI ethics teams, and fund conferences and research chairs at public universities.[10] For example, Amazon is a corporate leader in terms of its spending large amounts of money on research and development on tech tools for instrumentalizing and exploiting its labor power (see our conversation with Milla Vodello, Amazon Worker Solidarity, pp. 125). While the research firepower afforded to Big-Tech companies in these efforts is breathtaking, industry forces also work to capture, construct, and contain any opposition to their strategies. Uber, for example, does this by paying well-known professors six-figure sums to produce favorable academic research at respected universities and even by hiring away scholars who had been critical of the platform's labor exploitation model. Finally, tech capitalists pour money into foundations that build networks of experts empowered to speak for the global internet, setting agendas, and turning the volume up or down on different conversations if not overtly directing findings. Despite Silicon Valley's long-professed cyberlibertarian ethos, Google has quashed internal dissent by firing researchers critical of the famously racist trajectory taken by the company's AI tools.[11] Whether it is pursued through financing, coercion, or network cultivation, tech capital has a research strategy—and it is dominant.

The tech industry's outsized control over academic research priorities is connected to an older, Cold War-era history of the military's influence on scientific knowledge production, particularly in the United States.[12] This proximity to power makes it difficult (and sometimes dangerous) for academic researchers to remain openly critical of the industries that are directly funding their labs and institutions. At the same time, labor movements in both academia and in tech have the power to subvert and shape research trajectories and organizing strategies. In their conversations with Capacitor Collective members for this book, Alex Hanna (Distributed AI Research Institute) and Kate Sim (No Tech for Apartheid) discuss the ways their training as graduate student union organizers shaped their organizing strategies at Google and beyond.

This suggests that while the research university emphasizes scholarly publications, patents, and major grants, researchers can help circulate knowledge beyond its confines. This may involve illuminating organizing histories and possibilities to nonacademics in tech and the general public through teaching, or even after leaving an academic position. Academic knowledge production can also cater to labor's needs beyond the university, contributing to tech workers' critical understanding of where they sit in relation to other workers historically, geographically, and hierarchically across the digital economy value chain.

The pressure of austerity budgeting within the neoliberal university makes digital labor an appealing site of investigation to academics. The research focus on new labor dynamics offers a way to justify the relevance of social science programs as they contend for waning budgets. Precarious researchers at para-academic nonprofits follow digital labor research trends to appeal to funders. In this context, researchers increasingly compete for a dwindling number of jobs with secure contracts. They pump up publication numbers and conduct studies of online workers with quick turnarounds and little time to establish trust, understand the offline contexts of work, or shape research questions that serve the communities under study. Academics are, after all, workers too, and subject to many of the workplace invisibilities, inequities, and indignities that are familiar across digital labor.

Updating the workers' inquiry tradition for digital capitalism requires that we reject the scholarly detachment that academic institutions encourage. Our effort to forge a different relationship between research and organizing is rooted in theoretical and political traditions that vigorously refuse the notion of objectivity in research, aligning instead with feminist, community-based, and participatory action research approaches. These traditions blend organizing with the research process and trouble hierarchical distinctions between researcher and research subject. Research conducted in these traditions aims to generate knowledge that is unambiguously political and confrontational; its researchers build bonds of solidarity against pretenses of objectivity. Feminist philosophers and sociologists have highlighted the situated nature of all knowledge, demonstrating the need to recognize and embrace one's position rather than claiming false generalizability. Among others, Patricia Hill Collins has theorized how Black women's experiences as workers—in households and in academia—grants them deeper insight into social structures and processes, as they must navigate that which their employers or more privileged others ignore or disavow.[13] Similarly, researchers are compelled to ask more broadly relevant questions when they are held to account through community-based participatory research methods.[14] Through inquiry, labor movements can also challenge ideological beliefs that reflect the values of the ruling elite—what the Italian Marxist Antonio Gramsci termed "common sense"—with counterhegemonic knowledge built on workers' embodied understandings and "good sense."[15]

These epistemologies demonstrate how a sense of where one stands—understanding the limitations and advantages of those positions—can yield more robust and reflexive knowl-

edge claims.[16] Such models of scholarly research emerged
from—and were influenced by—social movements, so they
are irreducibly partisan and committed to methodologies of
solidarity. As we research across the myriad divides capital's
composition forces upon us, these radical scholarly traditions
have emphasized reciprocity against extractivism.

Building from these approaches, a digital workers'
inquiry must be rooted in collaborations with digital workers
and their organizations, challenging and breaking through
the divisions which artificially separate researchers and workers.[17] These perennial problems of anticapitalist organizing
and research are now playing out on a different terrain of
working-class composition. When Gramsci theorized the
division between intellectuals and workers, overcoming it
was exemplified by militant intellectuals meeting workers
in front of the factory gates. Today, we deal with new fractures: the divisions between academia and tech, between
permanent and precarious, and between labor aristocracies
(e.g., programmers) and low-wage workers in food service,
cleaning, and care industries.

Organizing across those lines of division can be powerful.
For instance, the Tech Workers Coalition (TWC) in Silicon
Valley originated when a cafeteria worker-turned-organizer
recruited an engineer to attend informal meetings among
other engineers organizing in solidarity with service workers to unionize on their tech campuses.[18] The movement
challenged tech libertarianism with a merciless analysis of
Silicon Valley's division of labor and the notion that even
the more glamorous and high-paid forms of knowledge work
can become precarized.

In the last decade, many workers and researchers have
built upon the tradition of workers' inquiry to produce powerful worker-led research fitting the material, political, and
social conditions under which digital capitalism operates.
In the UK, scholars have brought workers' inquiries into

call centers and across the metropolitan workspace of food delivery companies like Deliveroo, combining research with organizing.[19] A team at the Distributed AI Research Institute (DAIR) has initiated a community-based research project with data workers from across the world taking the lead in inquiries about their experience, struggles, and organizing efforts.[20] In Scotland, activist academics and labor organizers have argued for the development of "worker data science," drawing attention to bottom-up practices of data gathering, sharing, and analysis.[21] These data-based forms of workers' inquiry have highlighted the diverse compositions and situated struggles of the global labor force feeding AI and moderating social media content. More importantly, through creative forms of expression and knowledge production in a wide variety of media—video and film documentaries, vlogs, online speaker's series, and zines—digital workers' inquiries attest to the persistent need to foreground workers' knowledge for labor empowerment and organizing.

Feminist knowledge production reminds us to be aware of our own positionality as researchers who are mostly based in the academy. While we can't overlook the many differences, there is a striking symmetry in labor conditions from the college campus to the tech campus. Beneath privileged campus veneers, contingent, subcontracted food service, custodial, and clerical staff facilitate the cognitive labor of so-called innovation reinscribing racialized and gendered labor hierarchies in both of these contexts.[22] Further to this, cognitive labor is itself precarious; in the last several decades, the shift from secure, tenure-track positions to part-time teaching roles in higher education has made academic labor increasingly comparable with other forms of "gig" work where temps, vendors, and contractors are not given the same benefits, resources, or security as their full-time employee counterparts. By taking a self-reflexive position and situating ourselves within these structural dynamics, researchers can begin to make sense of digital capitalism's broader terrain and develop projects that strengthen the power of workers.

MAPPING THE SOCIAL FIELD

Digital capitalism remains, at the end of the day, capitalism—but to address workers' needs under digital capitalism, we must understand how modes of production have changed in the last decades. Platforms have become a new, highly centralized and data-intensive way of designing the labor process and generating data as intangible property and for the purposes of surveillance. Nick Srnicek notes that they constitute an extractive apparatus for data.[23] Fueled by vast sums of venture capital and boosted by powerful network effects, platforms have enabled firms to commodify data and gain monopoly power within industries ranging from advertising to e-commerce, food delivery, music, and data storage. As controlled, branded environments marked by hyper-surveillance, platforms are also social spaces that shape the nature of work in the twenty-first century. For example, Amazon Mechanical Turk uses machine-learning algorithms to monitor workers' "suspicious" behavior, suspend them, and lock up their earnings without due process. Uber and Lyft drivers similarly complain of algorithmic account suspensions, which amount to automated firing. Therefore, understanding platforms is critical not only for the insights into how digital capitalism operates, but how it might be—and how it *is*—resisted.

Often, the digital economy's workforce needs first and foremost to know itself. Platforms tend to function by organizing a geographically dispersed workforce, keeping it divided from itself in the labor process, and capturing and privatizing the results of complex cooperation processes mediated and structured by digital technology. Take Amazon Mechanical

Turk or any other type of online data labor—for instance, data labeling and tagging for machine-learning software. Workers may reside in any part of the world and will likely never meet each other. This digital mediation obscures workers' embodied presence and the geographies they inhabit.

But this atomization is not simply a byproduct of technological change; it is entirely by design. Even when workers are physically close to each other they can be kept separate. At Google, food service workers use a separate entrance to the building (see our conversation with Tech Workers Coalition organizer Erik H, pp. 105) and the secret "ScanOps" workforce—a group of mostly women and racialized contract workers who undertook the highly physical labor of scanning texts for Google Books—worked in a separate building and were discouraged from speaking to other workers at the Mountain View campus.[24] All along digital capitalism's value chain, workers are hidden from each other by brick walls and digital veils, even as their work becomes increasingly connected and interdependent.

In any industry, capital strives to deploy this process through subcontracting and outsourcing, reliance on individualized contracts and labor relations, and the imposition of individualistic and competitive workplace cultures that fracture the workforce. *Operaismo* called this process *decomposition* and strove to identify forms of recomposition that allow for workers to come together and face capital as a unified class. A digital workers' inquiry must figure out ways to overcome such artificial separations and study the social composition of the workforce beyond the political and technical obstacles set up by digital capital. This means illuminating the diversity and intersectionalities of the digital workforce, identifying common threads, and devising ways of learning, socializing, and organizing that can forge unities.

Efforts to build knowledge from below within digital capitalism start from the need to make work visible, and thus from the question of who and where the workers are, including their position along lines of difference with regard to gender, race, geography, and dis/ability, among others. AMT is again a perfect case in point: workers congregate in online forums maintained by workers themselves, where they share information, show newer workers the ropes, create supportive friendships, and produce research to understand their composition. One worker, known on the platform as "Clickhappier," published a meta-analysis of studies of Amazon Mechanical Turk worker demographics conducted by academic researchers across many fields, for purposes of understanding their workforces and study pools, but those academics had not made their investigations and results open for worker participation, feedback, or use. Their published works resided behind paywalls. Clickhappier compiled these studies to understand workers' education levels and national locations, finding that the majority were college educated. This finding flew in the face of stereotypes of Amazon Mechanical Turk workers as "unskilled."

Workers and allies develop community data approaches to help them gain power in the platform. Built in 2008, Turkopticon is a system created by white-collar tech students and Amazon Mechanical Turk workers to complement workers' research and forum maintenance capacities. The software allows workers to quickly exchange information, such as writing reviews of employers or "requesters" on the Amazon Mechanical Turk system and accessing other workers' reviews when choosing jobs. Eventually, this generated enough pressure to force Amazon to add an indicator about what percentage of jobs an employer has historically paid for.[25] Other kinds of data-driven research from below strive to reappropriate the data extracted and monopolized by digital platforms, in some cases repurposing the methods used by capital to automate algorithmic data analysis. The "worker data science" initiative developed by the Workers'

Observatory in Edinburgh aims at subverting the collection and analysis of digital information so that workers' existing practices of data gathering, sharing, and analysis can be collectively repurposed and supplemented with researcher expertise to gain insight into working conditions, pay rates, and managerial practices.[26]

Workers' inquiry can take the form of data collection or research document production, but it can also simply be a set of conversations that build solidarity across groups of workers that corporations do their best to keep separate.[27] In the early years of the Tech Workers Coalition, workers' inquiry took the form of an alternative ice breaker (see our conversation with RK Upadhya, pp. 89). At monthly meetings, new and old members would form small groups to discuss what they were doing at work, how what they were doing contributed to value production, and what were their grievances and frustrations with this work. Through these conversations, workers built relationships, analyzed class composition, and laid the groundwork for campaigns.

Media-making can play an important role in broadening the impact of these conversations. In harmony with the group's inclusive, solidarity-based approach to who counts as a tech worker, Tech Workers Coalition developed a publication, the *TWC Newsletter*, which has highlighted the experiences of cleaning service workers at Twitter, craft sellers on Etsy, contractors and temps at Microsoft, and food delivery workers at Instacart. In a section called "The Worker's Perspective," the newsletter features essays that result from a deeply collaborative interview and editing process with workers. These first-person narratives from workers across the tech industry create space for connection and solidarity, linking individual experiences to broader organizing movements. Similarly, researchers at Collective Action in Tech, Distributed AI Research Institute, Collective Action School, and Data & Society collaborated on a zine documenting creative workers' on-the-ground experiences with generative AI as a counterbalance to the hype and speculation around AI's future labor impacts. Organizers then used that zine to facilitate conversations with tech workers and researchers.[28]

In the face of digital technologies and contracting out, digital workers' inquiry can also assist organizers in mapping the workplace, an essential part of any union campaign. In Toronto, organizers with the successful Foodsters United campaign to organize Foodora delivery riders were forced to grapple with the reality that the city itself was their workplace, and that nobody knew how many people actually worked for the platform. Organizers met coworkers, had stoplight conversations, and got them to sign union cards at busy intersections.[29] Research carried out through the Capacitor Collective project assisted the Alphabet Workers Union with an unprecedented survey of Alphabet's contractor workforce, using data visualization tools on the company's own internal messaging systems.[30] The survey highlighted the volume of contractors used by Google, enormous differences in remuneration between Google's in-house and contract workforces, and how inequities among temps, vendors, and contractors are exacerbated by race, gender, sexual orientation, and ability.[31]

In China, taxi drivers in Shenzhen used social media groups to organize themselves into cooperative fleets, through which they shared information about job allocation and surge pricing and how algorithms mapped onto the city, as well as tacit knowledge to exploit the algorithmic loopholes of ride-hailing platforms (see our conversation with Qi Ge, pp. 137). Wei Ding argues that these drivers have recreated their knowledge about the workplace to challenge platforms' technical enclosure.[32]

Digital workers' inquiry involves understanding that the composition of the labor force isn't only about knowing who the workers are or mapping their experiences in creating value across the digital economy. Workers and researchers also need to get under the hood of the technologies designed to control them on the job and defraud them of the value they create. To do this, they need research.

ANALYZING THE TECHNOLOGICAL LAYER

The algorithms used to manage workers are famously opaque. Although workers encounter algorithmic calculations throughout their daily activities, these procedures are run at the deeper levels of the technological layer and according to logics that are inaccessible to them. They are "black-boxed" technologies. The software systems that run the show are proprietary, patented, secretive, or simply too complex to be analyzed and clearly understood. For instance, how is the price of a ride calculated? Why is a certain commodity assigned to a certain picker in a warehouse? What leads an AI tool to generate a specific picture in response to a designer's prompt? Which data have influence in a ratings system? A ruthless form of "epistemic injustice" enables the unequal distribution of power between workers and employers.[33] An inability to understand the "calculative logics" that underpin algorithmic systems is a defining feature of the conditions faced by the digital workforce and of its technical composition.

As noted by researchers facing such challenges, engaging these software systems requires taking opacity as one of their defining features. Social research has come up with strategies to study black-boxed technologies, for instance, through analysis of the documents corporations make available to the public, such as instructions, patents, or PR materials.[34] Yet digital workers' inquiry is uniquely positioned to "peel back the black box"[35] of algorithmic systems. Collaboration between researchers and workers can produce powerful tools to understand black-boxed algorithmic technology. Worker knowledge—the lived experience of workers—remains key to analyzing the labor process and the technologies used to organize it. At the same time, researchers trained in the analysis of digital technologies can provide priceless insights to workers who encounter such devices in the course of their work.

Attempts at generating knowledge from below surface organically when workers are confronted by opaque technologies. For instance, in many industries, workers have set up informal spaces for knowledge sharing. Having resources in common to navigate the apps or software that mediate one's labor can be vital when these tools provide so much power to management. Both Uber drivers and Amazon warehouse workers rely on massive Reddit forums to post anonymous information about their lived experience of the apps or inventory systems they work with. Facebook forums have become important resources for delivery workers at companies such as DoorDash who need to make sense of algorithmic logics such as price surging, ride assignment, or deactivation, so that they can collectively decline exploitatively priced jobs and give themselves a raise. WhatsApp chats were crucial in the cycle of labor struggles that swept the platform-based food delivery sector in Europe and beyond.[36] In these informal spaces that have been set up for similar app-based companies, not only in food delivery but in the service economy more broadly, workers can find app data, screenshots, and reverse engineer algorithmic logics based on the lived experiences of their colleagues.[37]

If these forms of organic information solidarity are key, how can they be enhanced by more structured interventions based on the systematic collection and analysis of worker data and knowledge? Rideshare Drivers United (RDU), an app-based driver organization in California, conducted a study in 2021 aimed at understanding pay scales and mechanisms in the local ride-hailing industry. They were assisted by the

Driver's Seat Cooperative, an organization that had developed an app that draws on the data collected by Uber from its workers. The data, analyzed by research think tank Policy-Link, showed that median driver take-home pay amounted to just $6.20 per hour in California, and was sometimes as low as $4.10 per hour. Thus, the study demonstrated not only that Proposition 22—a law introduced in 2020 that denies California drivers full labor rights—was substantially harming driver pay and access to benefits, but also that the process of algorithmic control was absolutely central in that process (see our conversation with Tyler Sandness, pp. 69). A similar initiative to better calculate the hourly pay of ride-hailing drivers was taken by the RideFair Coalition and the Rideshare Drivers Association of Ontario in 2023–2024. Analyzing ninety-six weekly statements submitted by drivers, RideFair concluded that the median hourly wage for drivers in Toronto was estimated to be C$6.37, much lower than the provincial minimum wage.[38] The drivers who participated in these initiatives were not mere subjects providing data to an academic study—they were engaged in a larger organizing drive that they contributed to envisioning in order to better understand their own working conditions and resist them.

Beginning our research from resistance does not mean ignoring how domination unfolds. Regardless of the methods used to approach them, technological artifacts—e.g., a piece of software or a robot—cannot be studied in separation from the managerial techniques that capital deploys to organize and control the workforce that operate them. For *operaismo*'s thinkers, exploitation is the result of capital's "rationality," which confronts workers in the form of machines, but also as all-too-human methods and organizational forms.[39] Early struggles in app-based delivery work aimed at exposing the human managers hidden behind the app. Studies of Chinese food-delivery platforms and AI data production suggest that human management's power complements algorithmic systems for labor control in order to contain labor grievances. This phenomenon captures the idea of "augmented despotism," which has been used to highlight how the technological organization of labor at Amazon warehouses—with its pervasive digital surveillance of labor—boosts managerial power rather than replacing or automating it (see our conversation with Mostafa Henaway, Immigrant Workers Centre, pp. 37).[40]

A digital workers' inquiry must ultimately seek a radical deconstruction and reverse engineering of the manifold ways in which technology and management work together to ensure capital's domination. At times, it is workers who control technology. In addition to repurposing or subverting the workplace technologies that capital relies on (like Slack or internal workplace mailing lists or messaging systems), one of the more intriguing developments within digital workers' modes of resistance has been the emergence of labor organizing platforms—the purpose-built, worker-to-worker communication channels developed by labor activists *for* labor movements. Turkopticon was an early example of these counter-technologies. A number of collaborations with designers and software developers have since generated digital organizing tools designed to be used directly in struggles, including the union-driven social networking site UnionBase, the "platform for worker voice" Coworker.org, and the AI chatbot-driven, question-and-answer app for and by Walmart workers, WorkIt.[41]

While this first wave of organizing technologies met with mixed success, they prepared the ground for a new generation of technologies which can supplement the face-to-face methods essential to organizing. In British Columbia, programmers have collaborated with unions to develop YouIn? This app was designed to help workers safely reach out to each other in organizing efforts.[42] Another example of these in-house organizing technologies is the Solidarity Tech app, designed in 2018 for use by Rideshare Drivers United in Los Angeles. In a conversation around the development of counter-platforms, the app's designer Ivan Pardo suggested that "software is more about how we build a process for turning intake forms into a conversation with somebody, [and] for turning intake forms into having a leader after a series of training sessions."[43] The tool allows driver-organizers to make encrypted phone calls, take notes, and rate drivers as potential leaders, activists, or supporters. While most Rideshare Drivers United members see themselves—not the technology—at the center of the organization's strength, the app has been key to overcoming gig worker atomization, enabling conversation and ongoing maintenance of the large amount of information necessary for large-scale organizing efforts.

These efforts to more fully understand the technological layer of capital's domination and even build parallel systems for the expansion of solidarity are ultimately directed toward an identification of the weakest links in digital capital's value chain. Here, too, things are moving, and the labor conflicts to come are becoming visible.

FINDING THE CHOKEPOINTS

If the aim of digital workers' inquiry is to produce knowledge that can be immediately used in struggles, it must go beyond understanding the working class and its exploitation to identify tactics to deploy against capital. Within digital capitalism, this often means finding ways to subvert, block, or slow down the algorithmic organization of production. Such a task can seem overwhelmingly difficult in today's thoroughly mediated and networked workplaces. How do you organize a union when your workplace is virtual and/or transnational, and you've never even met any of your coworkers in person?

How do you strike against a company which can easily reroute production through a different set of warehouses? How can you build worker power at a company where Slack channels are monitored and many of your colleagues are either depoliticized or afraid of getting fired?

At first, workers' intimate knowledge of the labor process in highly automated workplaces may be repurposed toward acts of individual sabotage and resistance. This can help workers subvert the global algorithmic organization of labor: in Italy, an e-commerce worker misplaces a commodity on the shelves, thereby gaming the inventory software that alone is supposed to incorporate knowledge of the randomized position of items in the warehouse; in China, a ride-hailing driver uses bot apps to circumvent algorithmic rules and reject ride requests paying low fares without facing consequences such as deactivation from the platform; in Spain, a courier learns to cheat delivery apps' facial recognition software and simultaneously log onto different companies and increase their chances to make enough money in one shift; in the US, a Google security engineer crafts a pop-up message informing workers who visit the website of a union-busting law firm about their legal right to organize.[44] These examples demonstrate how individual resistance practices can quickly turn into tactical weapons.

The very same knowledge can be harnessed to feed recomposition efforts and struggles when workers build mutual-aid systems or organize as a collective. In Canada, groups of Amazon workers and allies have been mapping warehouses in a metropolitan area to identify the chokepoints within the algorithmically organized network of facilities the company uses to reroute orders. The e-commerce company famously relies on a redundant network so that any disruption in a single facility cannot threaten to shut down the entire operations. The Canadian effort has not yet led to mobilizations, but in a similar attempt in Italy in 2021, a strike across the entire production chain—from call centers to warehouses and all the way to local sortation facilities and last-mile delivery—exposed the bottleneck represented by delivery. While the political goal of the strike was to make visible the national division of labor that e-commerce relies on, another result was the accumulation of knowledge about the strongest tactical link in this recomposition: drivers, who by withdrawing their labor were able to prevent the delivery of tens of thousands of orders in Milan alone.

Similar forms of grassroots knowledge production that feed struggles directly are at play in strikes or other mobilizations organized by app-based workers. One common strategy has been to use a collective, grassroots analysis to subvert the temporalities of digital capital. Workers, especially in the food delivery and ride-hailing industries, log off en masse from the app after having accumulated enough knowledge on *when* it would be best to strike, for instance, at the most profitable time for the company. Similarly, food delivery workers in many cities have organized to accept and then cancel orders from popular restaurants to maximize the effect of a labor action carried out by a minority of the employees. This knowledge is not built through a concerted research effort (although in some cases militant researchers were embedded in these groups), but rather, on series of informal and collective conversations—including sharing app screenshots of price surging and other app dynamics.[45]

Others have focused their efforts on subverting the artificial divisions through which digital capital separates and decomposes the workforce. For example, Uber's algorithms are designed to keep workers from meeting each other. To counter this, app-based drivers in Los Angeles and Washington, DC have taken advantage of their location at the airport to organize locally, repurposing the algorithm's logic of producing "just-in-place" workers.[46]

At times, the bottleneck is a symbolic one. The major walkouts organized by Google workers across the globe in 2018 to protest the company's labor practices and, most importantly, its response to workplace sexual harassment, highlighted this. The action represented a major blow to Google's public image as one of the most desirable workplaces for the tech workforce, with its aura of informality, horizontality, and creativity. Google had already removed its original "Don't Be Evil" motto, but to many, learning of widespread labor issues came as a surprise. While the walkouts were not the result of formalized bottom-up knowledge production initiatives, they did catalyze and inspire workers to use their lived experiences at Google as the source of narrative forms of inquiry. These sometimes took the form of intimate and self-reflective memoirs, such as Wendy Liu's book *Abolish Silicon Valley*. While women's personal essays are often diminished and derided, here they successfully exposed the structural inequalities embedded in the tech industry.[47]

Chinese tech workers had similar goals when they called out the tech industry's rampant overwork culture and mobilized a GitHub-based online movement called 996.ICU. The name refers to "work by 996, sick in ICU," an expression that captures the sector's typical work schedule: from 9:00 a.m. to 9:00 p.m., six days a week. This anti-996 movement attracted attention from the Chinese state and tremendous support from the domestic and international tech workers, pressuring some tech companies (e.g., ByteDance) to announce changes to its workers' schedules. Notably, Chinese tech workers repurposed the issues page on GitHub—typically used for technical troubleshooting—to share their workplace grievances. Although the anti-996 movement subsided not long after tech workers outside China showed solidarity, and the threat of layoffs loomed large in the slowdown of tech sectors within China, it shined a light on the poor work conditions highly skilled professionals face in the underbelly of the global tech industry.

WHAT ABOUT UNIONS?

Digital workers' inquiries bring researchers into regular and close contact with unions, raising political, ethical, and methodological questions about our relationships with these organizations. On the one hand, as institutions which unquestionably bring about tangible benefits to workers and lift them up through the power and resources they dispose of, unions deserve a default position of strong support and collaboration. While a significant amount of organizing within digital capitalism has been enacted by self-organized groups of workers like the Amazon Workers Union, Turkopticon, the African Content Moderators Union, and Rideshare Drivers United, established unions have been present all along the value chain as these flare ups have emerged.

On the large US tech campuses, outsourced cleaning, food service, and security workers launched a labor revolt through successful organizing drives with UNITE HERE, Teamsters, and Service Employees International Union (SEIU). Workers at cultural production platforms like Kickstarter and Bandcamp have organized through the Office and Professional Employees International Union (OPEIU), and those at Google chose the Communications Workers of America (CWA) to support the emergence of the Alphabet Workers Union. Temps and contractors at the Google contractor HCL Technologies organized through the United Steelworkers (USW) in Pittsburgh.[48] Similarly, in app-based platform work, established unions have organized food delivery workers in Toronto, while e-commerce workers at Amazon have been organized by CGIL in Italy and GMB in the UK, among many others. Unions have been catching up with some of the issues faced by the new workforces that make digital capitalism possible. In the process, they have also generated their own knowledge about the digital economy, often through union-led research departments or various "Future of Work" research initiatives focusing on the impacts of new automation on the workforce.

Despite these important contributions, to paraphrase the Zerowork Collective, a digital workers' inquiry should never mistake digital labor with its official organizations.[49] The traditional labor unions that emerged in the twentieth century are not the natural nor the only form of representation for workers. As institutions situated within capitalism, unions have serious limitations both historically and today. They are contested terrain, where rank-and-file members and bureaucracies are often in tension with each other and within themselves.[50] With their tendency to focus on bread-and-butter issues, established unions can neglect the broader objectives of worker control and anticapitalist organizing. US labor activist Jane McAlevey described how much union activity since the 1990s has happened within a professionalized "mobilization model,"[51] in which workers serve mainly as props in highly coordinated and mediated campaigns managed by professional union staff. This top-down approach has reached peak form with the rise of platform work, as some unions have agreed to maintain systems of misclassification in the rideshare and app-based delivery industries, in exchange for the opportunity to expand their ranks and generate revenue while avoiding the challenges of democratic organizing processes.[52]

Bringing the spirit of Zerowork to digital capitalism, one goal of a digital workers' inquiry is therefore to better understand the emergent relationship between digital workers and the trade union movement—when it is functional for workers, when it is dysfunctional, and when routing around it entirely is the only way to develop effective worker-led organizations. The picture is even more complicated by the structural constraints faced by workers in sectors (e.g., care work) and countries (especially in the Global South) where trade unions are simply absent or do not represent the main organizational form for labor. In these cases, grassroots knowledge generated by workers can be even more essential for organizing in the absence of unions.

Ultimately, although many instances of worker-led research that we identify as digital workers' inquiries have emerged in collaboration with unions and their research efforts, a digital workers' inquiry always maintains a position of autonomy with respect to unions. This position not only leaves open space for collaboration with democratic and member-driven initiatives by established trade unions; first and foremost, it maintains a commitment and duty of care to the workers without whom no successful inquiry would be possible. The goal of digital workers' inquiry is not worker representation. It is building *counterpower* so that labor can prevail at the negotiating table—or in open conflict—with owners. This approach to inquiry highlights the ways direct action and radically democratic forms of organizing can move us toward worker power. An inquiry-based practice that emerges from and supports struggles can build autonomous relationships with workers through the process of research itself.

OF ALLIANCES AND FUTURES

A digital workers' inquiry is in continuity with a long tradition of militant labor research, in both Europe and North America, but also arises from more recent transformations that have swept through academia and capitalism. Foremost, these include processes of restructuring, precarization, and the platformization of work under digital capitalism; but also more general processes of globalization, neoliberalism, and austerity; renewed offensives against organized labor; new forms of surveillance and political repression; the global emergence of new forms of fascism; advanced forms of climate change; anti-immigration policies; transphobia; and the spread of war and genocide. Because digital workers' inquiry is not a research method but rather a political approach to the production of knowledge from below that operates within and against digital capital, it cannot be imagined outside of the current historical moment with all its constraints and opportunities. Indeed, the new political formations that make digital workers' inquiry possible increasingly intersect and ally with movements against the use of computing in apartheid and genocide, immigrant surveillance, and climate destruction. In the US, India, Hungary, Italy, Brazil, and too many other places, they also fight against the resurgence of fascism and its impact on labor politics.

Importantly, digital workers' inquiry is not a technological determinist approach. While it focuses on the role of digital technology in mediating, organizing, controlling and—at times—liberating labor, it does so with an awareness that technology is one element of contemporary capitalism and forms of resistance against it. This point is important to workers, as they often find social science's fascination with technology problematic. Most would rather discuss the structural and material issues that have an immediate impact on their lives, from contracts to managerial despotism. Further, the technologies workers encounter daily on the shop floor often appear to them mundane and unimpressive. Digital workers' inquiry—whether focused on the algorithmic organization of labor, or the forms of sabotage workers adopt on the shop floor, or a subversive use of digital data, or the recomposition of workers' identities and struggles—is always aimed at producing knowledge toward collective liberation, not just knowledge for its own sake or for the rewards of academia. This orientation must be reflected throughout the research process and the ways its results are written up, shared, and discussed.

Researchers are predisposed to alliances with the digital workforce given the similarities we face across the division of labor in advanced capitalist economies. Academic workers might hire platform workers to drive their Ubers, annotate their research data, or deliver their late-night food. More precarious academics, such as graduate students and adjunct professors, may turn to platform or data work to supplement declining wages and job security in academia. These overlaps create possibilities for solidarity. Organizing and political education can help us, as differently positioned workers make sense of shifting material conditions that we sometimes share.

We share many common antagonists, too. Labor history is filled with examples of small groups of committed organizers struggling against the ways that owners, bosses, and the culture they produce pit workers against each other. Under digital capitalism, white-collar tech workers stand with cafeteria workers and Turkers engaged in collective struggle. Faculty organize alongside service workers on the university campus. How can our contributions to workers' inquiry illuminate the value chains that both divide and potentially unite workers in tech? How can research illuminate possibilities and barriers toward solidarity? How can it help us develop tactical and strategic knowledge for organizing?

Communication models within digital workers' inquiry must address concerns from all sides: who can speak for a group of workers? Whose names are on publications or reports—that is, whose knowledge counts and is recognized in public? What is the value of opaque and inaccessible communication systems such as scholarly journals and conferences if they confer legitimacy to academic knowledge, but workers cannot benefit from them? We don't necessarily have the answers to these questions, and we certainly do not purport to offer the definitive word on research best practices, but we hope that other researchers and organizers in this field will continue our method of centering workers' experiences and priorities.[53]

Even deeper epistemic concerns are on the table: think of the tension between providing authoritative knowledge that is valued by workers, and on the other hand, producing that knowledge through one's own positioning and worldview *as a worker*. An uneven division of labor based on class, gender, and race will tend to surface within the practice of digital workers' inquiry. Researchers must be ready to mobilize their privilege whenever useful, while at the same time working actively to undermine it. For instance, using someone's life experience as an example of a larger theoretical problem can be seen as an extractive practice and thus compromise the mutual trust that is so central to workers' inquiry. At the same time, it can help generalize workers' consciousness of their conditions of work beyond the individual experience (see our conversation with Mikaiil Hussein and Peter Zschiesche, United Taxi Workers of San Diego, pp. 79). Relationships rooted in solidarity between digital workers and researchers can help navigate the choices around representation in digital workers' inquiries.

Above all else, workers do not like being portrayed as passive, deskilled, or downtrodden. Research that uses employment situations as examples of dystopia tends to overlook the fact that people's working lives are also active, hopeful, and dynamic. This is one of the main insights of *operaismo*: workers and their struggles are major engines of economic change, whether capital likes it or not. A digital workers' inquiry is focused on workers as transformative agents. Thus, it can produce new ways of imagining different, revolutionary futures based on workers' empowerment rather than immiseration.

Worker-centered attempts at imagining such different futures can lead to radically new narratives. A lively example of this is *The World After Amazon*, a collection of speculative science fiction stories written by rank-and-file workers at the corporation. Here, workers "dream their own dreams, and reclaim the collective power to shape the future" in opposition to the dystopian plans Amazon has in store for its workforce, as put by the researchers who catalyzed this initiative. Stories include an alliance between humans and robots that sets off an uprising, or a woman's journey from terrified house cleaner in a post-apocalyptic gated community to fearless revolutionary.[54] Engaging in a digital workers' inquiry is different from writing a work of speculative fiction, but it can also contribute to imagining radical futures centered around workers' desires and struggles, futures that we hope will soon materialize to subvert and ultimately replace digital capitalism. In a period where digital capitalism feels ubiquitous and insurmountable, documenting workers' perspectives across the value chain may help foment new shared organizing strategies.

PART 2

MOSTAFA HENAWAY

IMMIGRANT WORKERS CENTRE (MONTREAL)

In conversation with Sarah Jean Salman

Mostafa Henaway is a Canadian-born Egyptian activist, a migrant justice scholar, and is currently a social justice fellow and PhD Candidate in the Department of Geography, Planning and Environment at Concordia University in Montreal. Mostafa's academic research is informed by more than two decades of organizing at Montreal's Immigrant Workers Centre (IWC), a grassroots organization that provides legal and political support to Canadian immigrant and migrant workers. He is an ally of many autonomous workers' movements both locally and internationally, especially in the logistics and e-commerce sector, and has become a leading voice for grassroots organizing in the digital economy in Canada and beyond.

In his 2021 article "Infiltrating Amazon"—based on his undercover role at a facility of the multinational company in the Montreal area—Mostafa circulated critical information about the work conditions in and politics of e-commerce in Canada. In 2023, his book *Essential Work, Disposable Workers: Migration, Capitalism, Class* was published by Fernwood, a Canadian independent publisher.[1] Around this time, social media studies scholar Sarah Jean Salman met with Mostafa to reflect on the role of research in workers' struggles and discuss the ways that current research can support labor organizing.

Sarah Jean Salman: Tell us a little bit about how you got involved in labor activism.

Mostafa Henaway: I was born and raised in Toronto, my father's a taxi driver and my mom's a school bus driver. I became active in social movements, primarily the antiglobalization and antiwar movements, at York University before I joined the labor movement on campus. I started organizing with taxi drivers around 2004 in Toronto over issues of misclassification—drivers not having the rights of workers—and that was done through the Ontario Coalition Against Poverty (OCAP).[2]

SJS: Your work with Toronto taxi drivers must give you a unique perspective on Uber and Lyft workers and their struggle?

MH: The taxi industry was in a way foreshadowing what labor relations have become—more generalized. Like, downloading responsibility, misclassified workers, this idea of "self-employment and autonomy." But at the end of the day, there are very big sharks that control the industry and its labor conditions—whether it be the city itself, garages, plate owners, and the banks that own the plate owners. Taxi drivers still have more autonomy and less surveillance than Uber drivers and slightly more freedom. But it's foreshadowed, not just by Uber or delivery platform labor, but by this idea of flexibility.

SJS: Could you tell us about the organizing at the Montreal Immigrant Workers Centre, and your role in that?

MH: When I moved to Montreal in 2007, I became active with the Immigrant Workers Centre (IWC), which organizes with precarious immigrant workers for both migrant and workplace justice by taking a movement approach and building leadership and capacity.

The Immigrant Workers Centre (IWC) was founded in 2000 by Filipino labor activists frustrated with traditional organizing approaches not recognizing the realities of immigrant workers. It started as a safe space for workers where they could build a sense of solidarity but grew over time within the Filipino community. Around 2007, we increasingly worked with textile workers who were experiencing mass layoffs with the offshoring of the textile and garment industry to the Global South. From there, around 2008, we began to see this change—the rise of temporary worker programs,[3] the structural use of agency work and temporary placement agencies, especially among immigrant workers. These two pillars became the focus of IWC until now.

IWC focuses on three things: first, on building collective campaigns, whether it be in workplaces or to change state regulations. Second, to do education and leadership development of immigrant and migrant workers. The third is to find ways to support those communities and workers, whether it be through legal clinics or labor rights workshops. That's really what we do; we're a bottom-up, hybrid community union.

SJS: I'm eager to hear about your doctoral work and how your experiences with the IWC influence that work. What got you into researching labor practices at Amazon?

MH: We had been working with warehouse workers for a decade. They were temp agency warehouse workers, and most were at Dollarama [Canada's largest discount retail chain], which is almost 100 percent staffed by agency workers inside their warehouses and distribution centers.

There were no Amazon warehouses in Quebec until 2020,[4] but we were fighting for justice around the same issues—high turnover, rates of injury, mistreatment, racialization of labor. These things were so pronounced in Dollarama that a slogan kept on coming up, "Dollarama is our Amazon." We kept on using it because nobody knew about Dollarama but everyone knows about Amazon. We didn't have many contacts at Amazon at all, and as a researcher, I thought, "Well, if Amazon is this future of labor relations, and the second largest employer on Earth, it made sense, if I care about warehouse workers so significantly, that my research be around Amazon."

My PhD work led to discovering that we had a bunch of contacts involved at IWC in previous forms and committees who were working at Amazon. From there, we got cases from Amazon too, from people who had been fired or injured.

SJS: Your experience infiltrating Amazon that you wrote about for *The Breach* was incredibly enlightening for understanding what Amazon workers and activists are up against.[5] What led you to that experiment?

MH: In 2021, I took a job at Amazon. The goals were to understand the model, how far reaching this could potentially become, and to compare it to other warehouses. Some things shocked me, some didn't, but if Amazon was going to be the standard of work, then there must be some form of regulation that could address that and could potentially affect all warehouse workers. Because e-commerce isn't going anywhere.

The aim was to say these are the jobs that are going to exist, and they must be better regulated because at this point, they're not. But through time, I've learned that a lot of things that Amazon does—it's very nebulous. They produce an image that hides the reality of what workers face. One of the aims was to unearth that and see what happens when you compare Amazon to other warehouses, seeing what workers feel is different.

SJS: Out of that, what's markedly different about Amazon's practices? How might you see those changing labor activism?

MH: A few things stand out. To rope workers in, to be able to extract workers' labor power to maximize labor power, it's not just brutal exploitation or "you won't find a job anywhere else" logic. Amazon tells its workers: "This is your family, you could be permanent, you'll move up the ladder, you could become a processing assistant, who knows, even operations manager one day. There are transfers, there's benefits, you'll be a blue badge."

They use this logic to draw workers in and keep them as productive as possible. If you're on the bottom of the chain, if you're a white-badge temporary worker, then you want to become a blue badge. If you're a blue badge, then you want to become a processing assistant. All of this is a draw.

At the same time, Amazon's model is to get rid of workers. You may see this anecdotally, but it's quantifiable. There's some statistics in the US about the turnover rate being 150 percent, but it's clear that Amazon tries to get rid of people between a year or two years of being there. They want workers to quit because they're just not as productive anymore. So, there's this false narrative that Amazon uses.

Other researchers have talked about this too, compelling workers through fear of the labor market, that "there are no more permanent and stable jobs." That's how Amazon really stands out—it's not because Amazon's nice and provides workers with benefits—it wants to get rid of workers. But you don't really see that until you're in there.

When you meet workers, the other remarkable thing is that, at Dollarama or other warehouses, there's not that ideology or culture. There's this blanket logic—you're a temp worker. You're here, you're not here. You don't like us? We don't like you. That's the unwritten social contract.

Another remarkable thing that workers don't care about as much as I thought they would is the so-called "technological aspect"—e.g., AI, or that your quota can be monitored. It doesn't register for workers how I thought it would. But if you say to those workers, "Would you accept that in public; being fully surrounded by cameras?" Obviously, everyone would be like, "No, that's not acceptable." But in the workplace it is.

The other thing is the opaqueness of Amazon; nothing is clear to workers. What's the management strategy? Who gets favored and who doesn't? Is there actually a system? It's a company with an automated HR system and it creates this tension between workers and management constantly. It's one of the bigger issues inside Amazon. And it flows from Amazon's ideology. I was struck by how much effort Amazon puts into creating this. It's almost a state; it has a whole internal regime of warnings, arbitration and care which confuses workers and makes them scared and angry.

Amazon claims it's a transparent process. But really, it's very smart because it just undermines the law. The real tools to arbitrate workers grievances locally is simply the Quebec Labour Standards, but Amazon has created this state-like apparatus. You can file internal complaints, use your own voice, appeal your warnings, all these things. It gives the illusion that Amazon cares, or your voice matters, but at the end of the day, it's just to get you away from using the law or your real rights. It's a unique part of Amazon's model.

Those are the key things that stood out the most working at Amazon. But also, despite its superiority and ability to dominate markets, how fragile the whole system is. Everything is on a thread because everything is regionally connected. Where the order gets placed and which fulfillment center it goes to and then which delivery station it goes to and then which route it goes through. All of that's minute by minute. If the trucks show up late, then the delivery station is backed up, and if the delivery station is backed up, then the drivers are backed up. The whole system is quite fragile because it's more lean than other logistics firms or retailers; this gives workers more power, but they don't see it.

SJS: How can we, as labor scholars and researchers, help in showing workers this power? What can we do better to support activists?

MH: To empower workers is to begin to show concretely, and not just anecdotally, that they're rendered to be disposable from day one. That's an important goal of the research because that breaks through Amazon's armor and ideology. Reinforcing that they're rendered to be disposable, that Amazon has no intention to acknowledge their rights. That they're not workers to Amazon—that, essentially, it's a laboratory. All these metrics, all these techniques are there to exploit them even further or render them useless. To shine light on things that workers feel—their individual experiences—and say no, those aren't just your experiences. You're right. This is an Amazon strategy. This is how they do it. And it's not just happening to you, it's happening to others, and we need to reinforce and support workers' grievances in academic work. Because those tensions are real.

    With Marx, that conflict between labor and capital takes place on the factory floor. Those feelings are part of the outcome of how Amazon extracts its profit. To dignify workers' experiences and their grievances is crucial. It's not just about what's happening inside Amazon, but the generalized impact of Amazon on other workers, because that gives an urgency to the activism inside Amazon. The "Amazon effect," if it's beginning to change labor conditions more broadly, is important too for academics, especially for those working on Amazon. It's not just what's happening inside Amazon anymore. Instead, it's how that's expanding outwards.

SJS: What do you think scholars can concretely do to engage in these conversations with workers?

MH: There's a view that workers are not intellectual. Like, the scholars are intellectual but the workers are not. That's a false divide. Why can't we have a political economy school, understanding logistics and the role of labor in that and gearing that toward workers? Some workers might show, others might not. But it's important for workers to situate themselves into something broader as this is what's going to give them power at the end of the day. To move them away from this individualized perspective. Are there ways that we could cowrite things to stress what happens inside Amazon is relevant to a larger public? What does Amazon's surveillance on the shop floor mean for society?

We need to be able to take that inquiry into a broader public discourse. We're cowriting a report with an advisory committee of Amazon workers on warehouse conditions. Workers did interviews, led surveys, and looked at the data, so they've been part of the process the whole time. Engaging with the workers makes the research more impactful.

SJS: Do you run into any challenges working as an academic in activist spaces?

MH: Yes and no. Sometimes, there's questions of accountability: is what I'm bringing into my writing reflective of what workers feel or am I simply extracting value from them for my career? I even ask myself that in a situation where I've used the funding or the space to work on Amazon to facilitate a group, to support workers, to fight their claims in court.

As researchers we can inspire, but sometimes we must think about how certain conditions for our research affects things. I didn't know this, but the article that I wrote for *The Breach*—which is not an academic article—was circulated amongst Amazon workers. That made me feel useful. Now, I recently published a long academic journal article, and workers are like, what is this? There are things academics might have to do to keep their jobs or to perform, but there must be commitment to making it useful to workers and organizers. It's not like going in, meeting people a few times, then leaving and writing something and it's over. It's understanding that same knowledge produced academically should be produced in a way that's useful for workers but also respects workers as part of that process and that knowledge comes from them.

Activists and organizers have spent years building those relationships, creating space for people who are willing to speak and meet with researchers. So, how is that work being respected or acknowledged? That's always a big tension. But that's overcome when academic labor is engaged in a real long-term way in these processes and projects.

SJS: What do you think scholars should ultimately learn from workers and activists?

MH: One thing I've learned throughout this—and there are real structural constraints, and this is the fundamental problem—It's not a critique of academics, because I'll just turn around and critique myself. But a lot of these things take time to play out, a lot of these dynamics and issues that could be interesting take time to really unfold. It puts emphasis on certain methods that allow for that.

When I began doing this stuff on Amazon, there was nothing. There were a few workers who began to organize the union . . . and then all these issues came up, and now there are these struggles. They take time, but obviously people have constraints. The university pressures you to publish so much every year, but we need to keep trying to find ways around the institutions that could allow us to do more interesting research, to allow time to play out in these struggles.

Another role for scholars: not to help workers understand issues, but to synthesize issues or reframe certain things without taking ownership of it. Being supportive and try to help understand the structural challenges and barriers to activism we face and how we might get around that, and not in a condescending way but by walking that journey with them.

The biggest way, and I haven't done this yet, is to find where we can copublish or coteach with workers, in a way that works against the academic schedule. Often, we find ourselves saying, "I can't do that because I have to write articles or I don't graduate," so it's about finding a third way. Accepting that, as scholars, we must go through the hoops and then find a third path that could allow for different engagement with workers that's related to that academic work, but outside of it.

SJS: Is there anything else that you wanted to share?

MH: A lot of researchers, even on the left, have this idea that it's distance that gives academics a radical perspective. Actually, the more distance you have from the ground and the activism, your analysis becomes more obscure, less rigorous and sharp. When you're grounded, it's much more work and it's tiring, but it enriches both the research and the activism. To fight against our idea of distance between what one is researching on and the researchers themselves, we must struggle against this idea.

ALEX HANNA
DISTRIBUTED AI RESEARCH INSTITUTE
In conversation with Enda Brophy

Alex Hanna is the Director of Research at the Distributed AI Research Institute (DAIR), an independent institute for community-rooted AI research. Since its founding in 2021, DAIR has been a key voice confronting the power and influence of Big Tech by documenting the way artificial intelligence is exacerbating racial, gender, class, and colonial inequalities.

Alex has long been involved with organizing efforts across the academic, tech, and nonprofit sectors, and has engaged in sustained conversations about the relationship between research and social movement organizing in the US and Canada. She has a background as an academic labor organizer and previously worked as a tenure-track faculty member at the University of Toronto. In her former role as a Google AI Ethics researcher, Alex led struggles against the silencing of critical voices within the company's AI arm during a period of intense employee organizing around military contracts, gender and racial inequities, and contract work at the company. In her letter of resignation after the firing of Timnit Gebru and Margaret Mitchell, Alex described Google as a company that "maintains white supremacy behind the veneer of race-neutrality, both in the workplace and in their products."[1]

Currently based in the Bay Area, Alex is a long-time collaborator and friend of several members of the Capacitor Collective. In October 2022, Enda Brophy interviewed her for a research project exploring the communicative dynamics of worker organizing at Google and in Big Tech.

Enda Brophy: You've had an interesting trajectory at the intersection of academia and the tech sector. Can you tell me a bit about your background and what brought you to activism?

Alex Hanna: My activist background starts as an under-grad at Purdue University, where I was involved in some Marxist reading groups as well as labor activism. My first political home was the United Students Against Sweatshops (USAS), which were campaigning around getting universities to stop using exploited labor in the manufacturing of university apparel, and with custodial workers and food service workers on campus. I was also involved in protests against the Second Iraq War in that political moment, which was really my political awakening in high school as an Arab person [*laughs*] living in the US post 9/11.

When I went back to grad school in sociology, I got involved in graduate worker organizing with the Teaching Assistants' Association (TAA) at the University of Wisconsin and became one of the copresidents of the union. It was the same year that the Republicans in the Wisconsin State Legislature decided to push through Act 10, which basically defanged all public-sector unions and that was really an intense year. Our union initiated the State Capitol occupation that lasted for three weeks, one of biggest protests that Wisconsin has ever seen.

So, I had a bunch of organizing energy until about 2012 and then kind of got burnt out and did some of my own introspection and came out as trans about a year later. I was doing some organizing around trans healthcare benefits for state employees back then. This continued when I became a professor at the University of Toronto, where I participated on the heels of many super-brave student organizers, especially against Jordan Peterson, who was a professor there and was then starting to become a public figure. I was one of two tenure-track trans faculty along with a number of contingent trans faculty and it was like, "Well, this is a great place to come" [*laughs*].

And then, in 2018 I left Toronto and went to Google, where I found a very vibrant scene of tech organizing, especially around Project Maven and the Women's Walkout that happened literally three months after I started. I got involved in organizing at Google around the Google ethics board that was disbanded within a week. The following year, Timnit Gebru was fired from our team. She had been our boss on the ethical AI team—she's currently my boss again at DAIR [*laughs*]—and so, after she was fired, I did a bit of organizing and writing, petitioning against Google's lack of accountability. That became very overwhelming and exhausting and so eventually I quit. That's my activist organizing history in a nutshell.

EB: That's a decorated record! You also did your doctoral work on tech and brought a critical sociological perspective into the tech sector. What's your experience doing research across these two worlds?

AH: Originally, I wanted to write my dissertation on Egyptian activism and social media in the 2011 revolution, but was a bit stymied by not being able to do research in Egypt because of the crackdown on researchers. There was a major chilling effect after an Italian student was killed in Egypt while doing labor research.[2] I mean, he was tortured and questioned . . . so, my dissertation became much more computational in nature.

I was focusing on using machine learning to study protest events. I was also realizing that while this was a methodological tool for generating protest event data, for instance from news reports, it could also be a tool for surveillance. I moved away from that work and started focusing on the ways in which machine learning could be used negatively. I learned about this idea of "algorithmic fairness and intersectionality"—I would call it "social justice and technology" or "social takes on technology"—and that was actually very helpful. That led into what I was doing at Google on the Ethical AI team, and that's what I've been involved in since I started my dissertation.

EB: I know a bit about the conditions under which you left Google, but I'm curious about your experience when you got there and how things changed. This was before your time, but my sense is the culture at Google really started to change when Larry Page took over in 2011 and it gradually became way more top-down and siloed. Was that your experience of the company?

AH: There was a lot of discussion about this when I was there. People were saying, "Larry and Sergei [Brin, the other founder of Google] are not around, you can ask whatever you want at TGIF."[3] There was a lot of questioning already happening around diminishing worker voice at the company. There were a few key activist listservs. One of them was the transparency and ethics listserv that I think emerged more from post-Maven activity.[4] It was moderated by organizers like Meredith Whittaker and Amr Gaber,[5] among others. Many of those people have left or have burnt out or have been silenced.

There was a lot of questioning about the growing restrictions on workers' voices at the company, including TGIF becoming an event that focused mostly on product and where you could no longer ask questions about the workplace. There were other ways they made communication technologies restrictive, like when they installed this community plugin on browsers that wouldn't allow you to invite more than one hundred people to an event. They kept adding more subtle restrictions on organizing technologies.

EB: Google is a company that has clearly stated its intention to organize the world's information. This requires a workforce that is tech literate and informationally savvy. Do you think this has had any impact on the organizing there? Is it like the sorcerer's apprentice, where you bring this tech-savvy workforce into being and then, hey, what are they going to do? They're going to organize through digital technologies. I'm interested in the communicative dimension of that organizing.

AH: I've thought about this a bit. Is there something about this firm that made it a more attractive site for organizing than Facebook or Apple or Amazon? Was there an organizational culture of permissiveness that made organizing easier? It seems like those organizations may be stricter toward organizing, even though at Apple, for example, there have been activists like Cher Scarlett, who is an outspoken person, and Janneke Parrish.[6] There have been activists at Facebook too. But is there anything about Google's culture, other than the way it used to encourage a kind of horizontality? I am not even sure that is necessarily the case. I mean, Facebook has a similar organizational structure to Google, so it might be the case that Facebook workers believed in the product less, given that it's had a lot more bad press and there's a lot less public trust in it. There were also people at Google who had been there for a while and did have belief in some of these principles and thinking the mission—making information more accessible—was pretty cool.

But the question you raised is about whether having this very knowledgeable workforce makes the company vulnerable to organizing, and I think it's sort of a double-edged sword. The individuals involved in tech organizing occupy a certain kind of social space. They're very intellectual, some of them see themselves as free agents because they could change workplaces relatively easily if they wanted, and this is especially the case for people who are very deeply technical. I'm going to use the example of the Chemistry Department at the University of Wisconsin because that was always the department we struggled to organize. It was a real problem. We'd try and organize grad students there and they would say, "I'm only going to be here for five years, I don't care about organizing, I make a lot of money because we're on soft money grants and they top it up with a bonus," you know? This is counterposed with the union strongholds of Sociology and English. In these departments at the university, people are not only there longer—seven, eight, nine, ten years because that's the nature of a social science or a humanities degree—these students are more easily able to see the casualization of labor because they tended to be paid the minimum on teaching assistantship stipends rather than grant money.

There is a parallel in tech worker organizing, where often you find people who don't see themselves being there for very long. I think at Google the average engineer's tenure is three years. So, they'll say, "Well, after this I'm going to jump to Facebook, then I'm going to jump to Apple." There's a much more open labor market for them and so exit is much easier. For instance, they can go to "start-up land" and make a bunch of money there, right? Look at who's organizing—sometimes they are program managers or they're the temps, vendors, and contractors who are treated like second-class citizens compared to engineers.

EB: So many parallels [*laughs*].

AH: Yeah, the analogue in academia could be grad student workers and contingent faculty vis-à-vis custodial staff and tenured faculty. There's a lot of parallels between the university and the tech sector and has a lot to do with how people see themselves as workers—as intellectual laborers. Some people might see themselves as above organizing or may think that in the cosmology of exit versus loyalty, exit is so much easier as a tech worker.

EB: I'm happy you raised the stratification across the tech workforce. I'm interested in your thoughts on the Alphabet Workers Union (AWU), with its "wall-to-wall," open union model that encompasses all Google workers, including those who are technically working for a Google contractor.

AH: I was 100 percent on board with the notion of wall-to-wall unionism when they expressed it, but I didn't really know about the organizing that they were doing for a while. There were a lot of problems with the organization. I mean, the model was Communication Workers of America (CWA)[7] coming in, ignoring the prior work done by grassroots organizers and really alienating a lot of the people that had been involved in organizing at Google for years. That turned a lot of people off from AWU. Anyway, I don't want to bad mouth it, but I also want to flag that there's a lot of ways in which that kind of organizing really demobilized a lot of people. Right now, I'm heartened that they've been supporting the No Tech for Apartheid campaign.

EB: Let's turn to the relationship between research and organizing. What should scholars who are involved with organizing keep in mind when they're engaging with labor activists?

AH: I think my initial thought is: what are the things that are going to be of concern to that community and how is this research necessarily going to support those ends? There are people who do a bit of writing on this work, and they might even share the politics of the organizing but are not involved directly with the community and do not really further discussions about what it means to form solidarity. What are ways of helping to further those goals?

I'll take the example of the Wisconsin uprising I was describing earlier. There were a number of sociologists who wrote about it, but some of that work kind of just stayed within academic journals. It felt like these people were just kind of piggybacking. Researchers should be asking: what does movement research look like? Often, movement research is not necessarily about looking at a movement's collective identity but rather, what kind of lessons can we bring in and learn about collective solidarities? How could this grow tech worker organizing? What can we learn from it? The extraction of knowledge is something we're also tangling with a bit at DAIR, where we're striving to center people who are not typically considered in AI development.

EB: What are some ways researchers can be accountable to the workers and the labor organizations they collaborate with?

AH: I think it depends. The structure is already unequal coming in. For instance, researchers often come in with some kind of funding.

I don't have an easy answer. I think accountability is really forged by establishing relationships that are long-term, that are deep. Ideally you have people that can kind of vouch for the commitments of scholars that do a certain kind of research. Some would say accountability is forged by ensuring that people are paid, that people are supported, that's one kind of way it can be approached. Although compensating people for their time doesn't guarantee the researcher's accountability because people may be less likely to call people in or note shitty behavior if they've already been paid, you know?

EB: What are some of the things or advantages that research can bring to organizing?

AH: I think there's a way of allowing space and allowing resources for people to do different kinds of analysis. For example, I think that analyzing who the target is for labor organizing can be helpful. I forget who said it, I think I saw Tamara Nopper tweet this, but I think she said something along the lines of, you know, "figuring out who's the target is the work." And there's a way in which research can identify what that target is and who to go after, because that's not super straightforward, right? Because it could be the state, it could be some high-level philanthropic organizations, it could be some family foundations, it could be a particular department, it could be an individual.

Some work that I'm doing with my collaborator Ellen Berrey focuses on universities, but universities are also a particular kind of organization that is very interested in entrenching a certain status quo, and because of that they're going to respond in conservative ways. So, some of the research we're focusing on is identifying universities' strategies of cooptation and demobilization, as well as the patterns of policing that they enact on student protestors and how that has risen at the same time as campus police organizations have gotten much bigger in the past twenty years, which is very understudied. So, I think there's a certain kind of analysis that researchers can bring that is helpful in identifying targets, really outlining how power is operating in a particular domain. And another way is just literally giving money to people who are already doing this analysis on the ground and saying, "Here, you're knowledgeable about this, let's go ahead and actually do the stuff that you keep on doing."

EB: Right, so contributions can range from the practical to the communicative. One of the traditions that I've been influenced by is the worker inquiry approach, or "co-research" as it's sometimes called, and the argument is that there should be an elimination of the space between organizing and research to the point that the research is the organizing and the organizing is the research. What are your thoughts around that kind of approach?

AH: The best kind of social research is one that is enmeshed in organizing, smart and actionable. However, they aren't necessarily the same thing.

KRYSTAL K AND PHIL
TURKOPTICON
In conversation with Lilly Irani

At the time of this conversation, Krystal K and Phil were organizers in Turkopticon, a worker-run organization advocating for better working conditions for all data workers. They are both longtime Amazon Mechanical Turk (AMT) workers, or "Turkers," a distributed workforce that performs online information tasks that cannot be automated in response to requests from clients of the platform. After reviewing this conversation during the editing process and reflecting on her own trajectory, Krystal, who is now a research fellow at the Distributed AI Research Institute (DAIR), stressed how some of her opinions in this conversation come from a position of privilege, as performing data work in the United States is very different from doing so in the rest of the world, and many workers do not have the same opportunities that American Turkers do.

Lilly Irani is a cofounder of Turkopticon, a software-based reputation system for Amazon Mechanical Turk employees powered by workers' reviews and commentaries. Turkopticon is a world-renowned example of the use of digital platforms for mutual aid that is centered around workers' needs and desires. In its first ten years, Turkopticon provided a space for workers to share resources, especially information about bad requesters. Beginning in 2019, a worker committee adopted governance of the Turkopticon project, and it expanded from serving as a hub for Turkers to share information about bad requesters and tasks to initiating organizing campaigns and advocating for policy changes. In November 2022, Turkopticon organizers led a campaign in response to Amazon mass rejecting Turkers and locking them out of their accounts without any explanation, creating a mutual aid fund for affected workers.

Lilly Irani: What have your experiences been as organizers for distributed data workers?

Krystal K: I transitioned from in-person organizing prior to Turkopticon to online organizing which has been a unique experience presenting unique challenges. I was brought onto this project almost three years ago. As far as this project goes, I've grown from someone who was very shy and not sure what to do into someone who wants to be loud and outspoken about bringing people in, helping Turkers realize they deserve better, and how they can use their voices to ask for better treatment.

Phil: I started working with Turkopticon about three years ago. I'd never organized before coming to Turkopticon.

LI: How did you start Turking?

Phil: I needed extra money. I retired to Spain and didn't want to use my savings. I've been doing it for about seven and a half years now. I enjoy it. I still Turk every day.

KK: I went back to school, and then I became sick and unable to do anything outside of my home, but I still had to pay my bills. I Googled online ways to make money from home and stumbled upon Amazon Mechanical Turk. I had never heard of it before, so I signed up. Then, I realized there were all these groups and resources and found Turkopticon. I started getting into it, and before I knew it I was able to keep myself afloat while I figured out my health. It was a lifesaver for me, and I still do it.

LI: Are there times when the work is stressful? For example, do you have any experience with mass rejection campaigns, when a requester rejects all work, which in turn negatively impacts Turker ratings?

Phil: I only work for about four requesters, so I don't get any rejections but I understand the problems with mass rejections. It's especially a big problem for new workers.

LI: What are you working on, in terms of limiting the mass rejections and their impact on workers?

Phil: We're trying to limit the amount to ten per day to limit the impact rejections can have on people's approval ratings. If your approval rating goes below 99 percent, what you can do on the site is limited. You can probably take the money hit—I'm not saying it's nice—more than the hit on your approval rating, because if it goes down you can easily ruin your chances of getting any work on the platform. You're penalized twice. It's not a fair system.

LI: Could you explain what is an "approval rating" for Turk workers and how rejections can affect them?

Phil: Every time you get a HIT [Human Intelligence Task] rejected, it works out as a percentage of the overall HITs that you've done.[1] Your approval rating will go down if you get too many rejections. Whatever rejection you get works out as a percentage. Some requesters ask for people who have an approval rating of over 99 percent or 95 percent to do HITs, so if you go below that you're unable to do most work on the platform.

It's not as bad for the long-time workers but getting a rejection makes you feel bad. It's a bad feeling, even if you've done it yourself by making a silly mistake. It's even worse when the rejections are not genuine rejections. Especially if you're new or you haven't done many HITs.

LI: How did Turkopticon organize around mass rejections?

KK: We started by reaching out to Amazon and saying: "This isn't fair but is something that can be fixed easily and we have some ideas." The person doing the task is not the only one affected. Newer requesters are impacted too. Suddenly, the work contracted out to AMT is done more slowly because Turkers become cautious. Especially after a huge mass rejection, people become scared. The requesters on the platform don't see their work suffer, but it takes longer to get completed and they're wondering why. Previously, people would speed through those HITs quickly. When we brought this issue to Amazon, we told them that this hurts the Turker, it hurts your good requesters, it hurts everybody—so why won't you change this when it's so simple to do so? They talked to us in circles, saying, "Oh, we'll put a blog post out." We're months past that meeting and no blog post has been published! It was like, "We hear you, but we don't really care." So, we took the next step to do this petition and proposed a limit of ten rejections per day.

Limiting rejections to ten per day is mutually beneficial for everybody using the platform. It's easy to implement. We received over 3,000 signatures from Turkers, requesters, and allies. We delivered the petition to Amazon and didn't hear anything back for a while until we got a second meeting. We sat through another meeting where they talked in circles to us and nothing happened afterwards.

We started looking at other ways to bring attention to this and decided to start a social media campaign to put pressure on Twitter and other platforms. We were searching for a journalist who would want to tell this story, and as we were doing this, the company AI Insights unfortunately fell into our laps. They were a new requester, with a great approval rating right off the bat, and they mass rejected over 70,000 HITs, affecting countless workers.[2] We don't even know the total number of workers affected by this mass rejection event in August 2022, but we've heard numerous stories on social media as well as through email replies to our newsletter.

LI: You've been doing a lot of research as organizers yourselves, with surveys for example. What was the process of researching the mass rejections campaign? What did you have to find out and learn?

Phil: Before we did the petition, we put a survey out and asked Turkers what they thought. We picked out seven or eight different things to ask for plus they could add something they thought was missing. Rejections overwhelmingly came back as the main issue with the platform. There are other issues but that was the main one.

KK: The survey was the beginning because we didn't know what the Turker community found most important. We thought we knew but I think some of us were surprised that it did come back as mass rejections. Then we took the next step and reached out to people who had mass rejections happen to them. Everyone's scared of the threat of mass rejections. It's a fear almost every Turker has, so we can see why it would be the number one issue, but are there people out there that have had this experience? Yes, there are. So, we got their stories and started moving forward, making sure that there was an actual workplace issue here and not just the fear of the issue.

LI: Your proposal to Amazon about capping mass rejections seems like it's also an outcome of a research process. How did you work that out? What did you learn? Who did you consult with?

Phil: Originally, it just came to me after a meeting. I said it out loud and played with the idea a bit. It moved from there.

KK: I remember that day because we thought, okay, what do we want to ask Amazon for? There are some rejections that are justified, and there are some people who occasionally try to scam the system. We wanted to make sure that the requesters who come on and do mass rejections on purpose--they reject the work so don't have to pay the workers but somehow still get to keep the data—are ones that were not justified. How do we limit the damage from that? Phil came up with the cap of ten. However, the cap doesn't mean that Amazon would have to turn around and pay for those HITs or do anything more than just implement the limit. This way good workers could keep working. It's such an easy solution.

Phil: You have to organize it in a way that is fair for everyone and the cap of ten is fair to everybody—including the genuine requesters and the Turkers.

LI: What are some of the ways that you've worked with research or researchers as part of organizing?

KK: During the whole process of getting this proposal to Amazon, this petition, we were doing informal research. We were taking input from the community, making sure that we're speaking to the people affected by this, and taking their opinions, ideas, and thoughts. This process has been well over a year, if not two years, in the making. It's been lengthy because we wanted to get it right.

Looking at it now, it parallels the research process in some ways. We read some of the academic research papers published over the years, noticed gaps or some things that weren't quite right, and thought about how to use them to our advantage and challenge what's being argued based on our experiences. I think we've used that type of research and expanded on it in our meetings. It has helped formulate some ideas.

Phil: One thing you do learn by looking at some of the research is seeing the kinds of things people aren't asking for or don't want out of research. For example, research that has been done on Turkers' hourly wages. One study in particular argued that we make around $2 or $1 per day. We knew for a fact that we would never want to research the topic [of an hourly median wage] but you see what other people think of it.

LI: How did the research about Turkers' median wages come to you? How have you understood and responded to that research?

Phil: Some of the research that's been done about Turkers doesn't include the involvement of Turkers. These researchers didn't ask the Turkers what they wanted or they assumed what Turkers wanted. For example, when researchers argue for Turkers to be "employed" but haven't thought through what that means or would look like.

KK: We stumbled across the research about hourly wages because we did our due diligence with the studies that exist out there and we looked at all of them. We wanted to see what researchers had to say about the Turker community. We found a lot of it to be inaccurate and some of it definitely brought about some harsh feelings while we were discussing it. With the hourly wage research, we found the research methods it used to be flawed based on our actual lived experience. The researchers for this study had asked Turkers to install a Chrome extension tracking usage. Only, we were able to find out, based on our own inquiry, that some people leave their computers on all night and might set an alert for one particular type of work. If it goes off, you get out of bed because you think you can make money. But while everybody's sleeping, this Chrome extension is still running. It was tracking those hours as working hours. So that brought the hourly wage down further.

There seems to be a narrative researchers use that characterizes Turkers as poor, impoverished, and unskilled workers who make $2–$3 per hour. Where being a Turker is equivalent to slave labor. This way of doing research, where you're tracking hours, seems to make it so that the results correspond to popular opinions about the poor, poor Turker. We found that to be troublesome because we don't see ourselves doing slave labor or busting our rears for $2 per hour. Nor do we see ourselves as being unskilled. We were bothered by this kind of research, and that fueled us to find other research that resonated more with our experiences.

That one study launched us into looking at different things while at the same time asking Turkers how they felt about that research. In our open forums—online spaces where Turkers can gather anonymously—we talked about this study. It's hard when somebody puts this narrative out there about you, but you know that it isn't an accurate representation of you and the community you're a part of. Working with research on that level has been frustrating as well as motivating. We've been thinking a lot about how we can work to change these narratives too.

LI: What are some ideas about how you can work to change the narrative about Turkers and make it something you all want?

KK: I had a conversation with one of the lead authors of that study—the one about using the Chrome extension to track worker hours and to calculate hourly earnings for Turkers—and tried to explain why it wasn't accurate. It didn't turn out very well. But for us to calmly say, "Hey, we've read this, we don't feel this represents the community," and to make researchers very aware that we're reading what they're writing—that has an effect.

We want these researchers to know what their research looks like from the perspective of a worker, how we work, and how we use this research to write our blog, newsletter, and social media posts. We want researchers to know that Turkers look at and read their work. Research like that can take the wind out of a Turker's sail very fast. To be told that you're unskilled, that you're not smart enough to make more than a couple dollars an hour, it fires people up. I think there's room for challenging those issues more than we have already.

LI: I like the idea of research that puts the wind under Turkers' sails.

KK: It's great when a researcher comes in and has knowledge of the platform and has used it from both a worker account and a requester account—but hasn't only used it for a week. There's plenty of research where the researcher says, "I signed up to be a worker, and I worked for a week or two weeks, and I made seventeen cents." Just like any other job, you don't start out knowing everything on day one. By day seventy, you still don't know everything. It takes time to learn the tools that help us do our work and the ways different things operate within the system—the good requesters, the bad requesters, how to maximize your time, and so on. To the researchers who come in and try to tell us about the platform despite only working on it for a week: if you want accurate research you need to go through the whole learning process of the platform.

Phil: With some of the research, it seems as if the researcher already has an outcome they want and do research to prove the point they're trying to make. Like, for example, the research on wages.

LI: What would have been a better way to approach researching Turkers' hourly wage?

Phil: It's an odd question; I don't know if it's research that would be useful to Turkers. You have to get the right demographic and you have to get people from different countries. You can't go to one country and then use that to draw conclusions for everybody.

KK: That's a great point. Some requesters I will never see. Let's say they're popular in India or Brazil and they pay significantly less for HITs. If you're trying to calculate an hourly wage and publish this paper on it in the United States, the wages may appear low based on average wages in the US. Folks in India, however, may have a different response if you ask them about whether the wages are good or not.

How do you have a minimum wage for Turkers if people are working all around the world in places with many differing minimum wages? Even in the US, the minimum wage varies by state. This needs to be considered but it's never even mentioned.

Let's go back to the example of the researchers using a Chrome extension to track Turkers' hourly wages. If you want to install a Chrome extension, that's fair, but are you able to design one that stops tracking after a period of inactivity? Should it be the Turker's own responsibility to be turning the tracker on and off if they agree to do the study?

One of the more alarming things I've seen is this how this article has created a narrative across a large portion of the community that's researching this. This study, and the researchers' flawed conclusions, are being cited in many other academic papers and journals. I don't think this study has been replicated, or I've yet to find another study that has tried a similar method to corroborate or disprove the results. It was taken as a fact and over the last few years it has been used repeatedly. That's alarming to me. I see this as a pitfall of research.

LI: In disciplines like psychology, researchers call that the "replication crisis." How can researchers be accountable to the workers and labor organizations that they collaborate with and need to learn from?

KK: It's a tough question. As far as being accountable to the workers, researchers, journalists, whoever it is, can't go and share everything they're writing with us for a number of reasons. That's fair, and I understand that, but they should take some time to speak with us. They might discover that some of the preconceived notions, or things taken from popular research, might not be accurate. Approaching us—and saying what their intentions are, what they want to accomplish, and how we can help and be a part of their research—would be helpful.

Phil: Be honest and true from the start about what you expect to get out of it and what you're looking to achieve rather than trying to play both sides. Tell people your goals.

KK: Be honest about the perceptions you already have. For example, you can say, "This is what I have in my mind, and I'd like to hear if you think that's accurate." Even if I was offended by the viewpoint they had prior to coming in, I would have the utmost respect for someone who was honest about viewing Turkers as being unskilled workers who work for $2 per hour and then asking us if we think they are correct, incorrect, and why we think that. That would be a dream. It's okay to have preconceptions about things prior to doing the research—but be honest about it and have an open conversation about it. This would go a long way in building trust.

TYLER SANDNESS
RIDESHARE DRIVERS UNITED
In conversation with Brian Dolber

Tyler Sandness is a former Lyft driver who became one of the members of Rideshare Drivers United's (RDU) organizing committee calling for historic strikes in advance of Lyft's and Uber's IPOs (initial public offerings) in the spring of 2019. RDU started in 2017 as a small collection of drivers organizing for higher pay at the Los Angeles International Airport (LAX) lot. Since then, RDU has grown into a self-organized, worker-run organization of more than 20,000 drivers throughout California fighting for labor rights and a union. Tyler became a paid staffer with the organization in 2020, and now works remotely for RDU from Tacoma, Washington.

Brian Dolber moved to Los Angeles in 2015, leaving behind a tenure-track faculty position in New York State to seek work as an adjunct lecturer. In need of both additional income and a next academic project, Brian began driving for Uber. While giving presentations in academic settings and public talks about platform work, he came to learn about and helped to build RDU. It is in this context that Tyler and Brian met.

Tyler played a key role in coordinating a study of drivers' earnings under Prop 22, the California law passed after a massive $220 million campaign by gig platforms that misclassified app-based drivers and delivery workers as independent contractors.[1] In this conversation, Tyler reflects on his role in the study and his views of the role researchers play in platform organizing.

Brian Dolber: Through your experience with RDU, what roles have you seen researchers play in contributing to the organization's mission?

Tyler Sandness: Academics are providing the "framework of truth," so to speak. What we're dealing with are giant companies that are incredibly obtuse about how their business operates. They do that on purpose. Unfortunately, I've also seen companies hire, or have relationships with, academics to create outcomes that are beneficial to the company's line. That's very unfortunate, and the danger is not that we hear so many lies that we mistake lies for the truth, it's that we hear so many lies, we can't even tell what the truth is anymore. I feel like academics who go into that line, where they are willing to arrive at conclusions beneficial to their patrons, are doing a massive disservice to academic research and ultimately eroding the legitimacy of the research.

BD: One of the things that we've been talking about, since publishing our study in 2022, is: how do we make these numbers real for workers and for people in general?

TS: I think that you need to really understand your subject if you're crunching data about it. The only way you're going to understand your subject is by talking with them. It's very easy to block people into giant monoliths and then talk about everyone's experience as if it's the same. We're talking about human beings—but, you don't really think of them as human beings, you think of them as a data point. Being able to really understand that the data point is a human being with an experience, perhaps with a family, or with struggles, having that connection enables you to better understand your subject and how this is going to be perceived.

BD: Have you seen any examples where there have been tensions or problems in working out those sorts of translations between numbers and lived experience, or theoretical-academic speak versus ways that maybe drivers understand things and experience them in their own terms?

TS: What comes to mind is—toward the end of the Prop 22 study, where the language of the report is academically rigorous but at the same time impenetrable to anybody outside of trained data scientists. It's just very difficult for people who don't have that toolkit to digest what they're reading there.

That's a constant tension between the organizer and the academic—where the academics need to have legitimacy, often of a field, and that means using field-specific language to be able to demonstrate to other researchers that this was done in a rigorous manner, it has legitimacy, and should be taken seriously. But that doesn't always translate well to the people who are being affected by the problem.

BD: How have you, or how has RDU, tried to ensure some level of accountability so that people are doing work that is supportive of the organization and not what we might call "extractive"?

TS: I think that involves being selective of partners. I think it means having a preexisting relationship, or at least a confident one, with the organization built up over trust. So, for example, my relationship with Victor Narro out of UCLA has been built over the past two years of getting to know him, working with him, and then trusting that he's interested in seeing RDU succeed as a project. Having that trust and then also having clear communication with them about what's working and isn't working.

I've had difficult conversations with Narro. At one point, we got sent interns who were not qualified for the work that we were doing, and I had to say that we needed to fix the process, to make sure that people being sent to RDU were eager to learn about organizing, that they were looking into careers in organizing, and that this would be experience they could take into the rest of their lives. One of the students we ended up with at this time was like, "I'm going into HR right after this." I'm not here to train an HR person how to fight unions, so being able to have clear communication and a relationship both parties want to maintain, has been crucial to maintaining that accountability.

BD: Can you talk about your role in the Prop 22 study?

TS: I guess I envisioned myself as a project manager for that first part of the study which was the actual data collecting. So that really was my role—helping to make sure that I was coordinating with the app team that we were using to actually collect the data, coordinating with the academic research team to make sure that the data was being sent out and the methodology was being followed, getting the drivers to actually participate in the study and then working with drivers to recruit and supporting them during their month of collecting the data. I did that by managing a small team of UCLA interns who every week would do check-in calls with all of the drivers to make sure the app is working and ask: are there questions that we have that are causing problems? Are there anomalies that are occurring on the road that we need to be aware of and troubleshoot for?

BD: So, you did a lot.

TS: I did. Although, I feel like I was very frontloaded, because for the second half of the project, I was just another voice in the room providing feedback on the study. Even though I have a bachelor's degree, this is where my lack of data science was a real hindrance because we're talking a lot about methodology, it's a lot of complex statistical math, and I just do not feel very equipped to be part of that conversation.

BD: What do you think you offer that conversation as an organizer and as a former driver?

TS: That is probably a very useful voice in that conversation. Accessibility needs to be a concern, especially in the public policy space. If people can't understand it, then people can't advocate for it. An organizer is always thinking about how we can present this to people in a way that is meaningful, that can help people reflect on their own experience and realize that there is something wrong, and then help guide them to the journey of understanding.

BD: You were in the room during a lot of the conversations about methods, the drafting of the methodology, and about whether those methods were capturing the reality of what it means to drive. How do you see that role as being fundamentally different from my role as a researcher?

TS: Your role, as researcher, is to process, analyze, interpret the data, and arrive at an understanding of what is really happening here. There's a bunch of complex tools that you have to elucidate and understand that. The conflict then, is how to take that understanding you've gotten and have that become something that a nonacademic person can comprehend, get agitated around, and then take action.

Our goal is to reflect—to give us an accurate picture of reality—and my goal is to take that further and say like, if that's what the picture is, if that's what we're really dealing with, then here is how we work together to solve this. I think academics can absolutely be advisors for groups like this.

Honestly, we all need advisors—people who understand the reality of what's going on and are able to provide their two cents. In organized labor, it should always be the workers who are in control; it should always be the people who are actually working there that make the decisions. But, you know, having that educated adviser who can provide accurate pictures and solid advice has been around as long as good governance has been around.

BD: What voices have not been reflected in some of the research that's been produced through or about RDU?

TS: Whose voices haven't been heard? African American drivers are poorly represented. I think that it's just more of a problem with RDU than it is a problem with the study. There are definitely communities that RDU could be doing a much better job of engaging with.

The issue is finding somebody who's passionate about what RDU is doing and can be that leader within their own community who brings that community into the bigger work that RDU is doing. There's so many ethnic enclaves in California that have not had enough representation within RDU, and so their voices are not included within the research. The African American community is one of them; the Asian American community is another. These are areas where RDU needs to improve, and by doing so, it would improve the ability for those voices to be elevated.

BD: That probably plays a role in what you were discussing about communicating the results to members. If it doesn't reflect the diversity of the driver base, how do you then reach back out and use this as an organizing tool within all those communities?

TS: It's a challenge, because we have drivers who don't want to accept what the reality is that you've laid out for them. Then you have drivers who simply view themselves as independent contractors; they view themselves as their own boss. And being told that you're not really a business owner, you know, it's a hard thing to accept.

BD: They're getting that story about their identity from, not strictly, but often, propaganda that's being deployed by the companies. That's the story that the companies tell. And they use "research" to back up that story and to perpetuate that story. So, in some ways, we kind of need to figure out how to use that data to tell a story that better resonates, that displaces the other narrative of independence and entrepreneurship, etcetera, right?

TS: That's the challenge of organizing. Organizing could use better ammunition to be able to have those conversations. Organizing really is about meeting a person where they are— not necessarily challenging them outright, and saying that what you believe is wrong, and you're wrong for thinking it, but rather finding what is the crack in their belief and how do you guide them to questioning it themselves. Because the defense mechanism automatically kicks in the moment that you tell somebody that they're wrong. What organizers need is enough ammunition and enough sort of proof that then gets the individual to question: well, why do I believe the thing that I believe? And if the thing that I believe is not correct because the data that I'm exposed to is showing the flaw in that, then what else may I not be right about?

BD: Do you have any thoughts about how we make sure that we can communicate to these different constituencies without reproducing those divisions?

TS: It's a very detached process. One problem with the system is that if all the mechanics of what's going on are happening behind the curtains then no one feels like it's real. Then the impacts come so late that it's difficult to make the connection of cause and effect between a policy being adopted then actually doing something to help people. Maybe it would be good to peel back the curtain a little bit and show how the mechanisms are working.

BD: Do you think engagement from researchers helps with curbing that sort of skepticism of the university?

TS: I think part of the problem is that working people do not feel like academia respects them. It feels like academia talks down to workers because they don't have the same toolkit. Not having the toolkit does not make you less of a person, it just means that you don't have expertise within the field. Holding your expertise over those people and assuming, "Well, I'm better because I'm paid more, and I've got this title, and I have this tool set," that doesn't make you inherently better. Do your best to take away that bias. Take away the feeling of superiority when you're talking to workers: don't talk down to them, be willing to speak their own language and respect that language.

BD: Are there other roles that you think researchers could play in helping RDU?

TS: Being in an advisory role—being able to connect the world of academia to working-class people and making the work they do real for working-class people—could be a massive boon for helping the establishment of new working-class institutions. That's something academia really needs to work on—one of the reasons we're in the crisis we're in right now is that working-class institutions have been dramatically eroded and replaced with something out of hell, so to speak. It's a vision of hell. You look at something—like, say the conservative project to create their own institutions on the other side, and that's been in direct response to the failure and destruction of working-class institutions that would otherwise provide other perspectives or a home for people to feel like they belong in civil society. Anything that universities can do to help support and develop working-class institutions and civil institutions to combat—not to be dramatic about this, but—fascist institutions within the country is something that needs to be taken seriously, to whatever degree is feasible within the universities. Otherwise, they will eventually become a target for what might very well be coming. Again, sorry to go down a dark path with it—but I feel like I'm in Germany in 1936 and it's time to start talking about that.

BD: There's darkness among us. Not just down the path, but it's already here, right?

TS: It is very much here. People wonder why didn't the German people rise up against Hitler, and you look around, and you're not seeing anybody standing up against Trump or these rising fascist institutions.

BD: Before we wrap up, do you have other things that you want to raise?

TS: No, I think that this has been pretty comprehensive. This is a message going out to your colleagues and academia at large, as well as to the readers of this book: don't abandon civic society. Get yourselves reengaged within communities.

MIKAIIL HUSSEIN AND PETER ZSCHIESCHE

UNITED TAXI WORKERS OF SAN DIEGO

In conversation with Lilly Irani

Mikaiil Hussein is the President of United Taxi Workers of San Diego (UTWSD) and Peter Zschiesche is a board member of UTWSD and founder of the Employee Rights Center, a worker center in San Diego. UTWSD is an AFL-CIO worker center that advocates for taxi drivers on public policy and regulatory issues. The organization is a community-driven transportation technology initiative emerging out of a half-decade campaign to make medallions more accessible to drivers.

Lilly Irani, an ex-Google worker and now a professor of communication at University of California San Diego (UCSD), came to know Hussein and Zschiesche through her work building a Tech Workers Coalition local in San Diego. They collaborated to codesign and negotiate a worker-centered ride-hail app called Ride United, developed with software partner Yamsol. PhD student and ex-Microsoft worker Udayan Tandon was central to these efforts, and many other UCSD students and Democratic Socialists of America San Diego volunteers made significant contributions as well. The aims of the project were to build an app that workers control as much as possible, identify policy and resource barriers to full worker control, and to inform a structural socialist agenda to make "real utopias" within capitalism possible.[1]

Lilly Irani: Tell me about the United Taxi Workers of San Diego (UTWSD) and how you became involved with research and researchers?

Mikaiil Hussein: I came to San Diego, lost my job, and started driving a yellow cab. My organizing started before I even got the job: I was waiting to be accepted when I saw this driver having issues so I decided to help him. He was Somalian and subleasing a cab. He worked a twelve-hour shift, but the boss said he didn't pay him to operate the cab, so they weren't giving him his money. The boss then blocked his number and name on the computer from accepting any calls so he couldn't work anymore. That's where it started for me.

Over the years, we continued organizing. There are a lot of issues in the cab industry that we have to deal with so we started working with a law firm to help us out with employee rights. They brought people in, like Sarah Sáez, an organizer who could advocate for us and had the knowledge to pinpoint our issues. We developed the Safe Cab San Diego initiative which eventually transferred to the Center on Policy Initiatives (CPI).

Peter Zschiesche: CPI was organized in the late 1990s as a pro-labor think tank for San Diego. The idea was to bring the expertise of academic research to the labor movement. Ellen Dannin was a professor at California Western School of Law (CWSL) and was one of the major people behind this. One of her specialties was the privatization of the public sector. When Sarah came onboard as an organizer, she learned about CPI. That's when we realized we needed data to analyze the present reality of the taxi industry so we could change it.

Mikaiil and Sarah were voicing the need for policy change and started connecting with people who knew that if you're pushing for policy change you need to have a report and present the problems of the industry.

LI: What is it about policy change that requires those reports?

MH: Our work is very overregulated. Once we mapped out the work process, we needed to study how much drivers were making, how long they've been driving, what the average costs were, and who was doing the work. We didn't have a voice in our industry, so we needed a report to bring a solution to the problem from the beginning.

PZ: The San Diego Metropolitan Transit System board (MTS), in order to back up its policy, does a market study to justify any caps on taxis to allegedly limit competition. Once we saw that, we realized we needed to get our own data to counter their arguments since MTS' report ignores the reality of workers. That's where our report, "Driven to Despair: A Survey of San Diego Taxi Drivers" came from.[2]

MH: We were not supposed to be at their table, in other words. So, we put masking tape over our mouths as one of our actions during one of their board meetings. Fifty drivers showed up and said, "we don't have a voice" to the taxi advisory committee. The board has nine representatives who are all owners of cab companies. There's one driver representative that's selected by the owners. At the beginning, we were learning how to even say something; we didn't even know that the public could access these meetings.

LI: Are there other stories you'd like to share about how you've been engaging with researchers?

PZ: "Driven to Despair" was the capstone because it became the central study for people sitting in city council meetings and the MTS board. It became the dominant description of the taxi industry in San Diego. The industry relied on being the institutional insiders so they just didn't have the capacity to create another study. Our study enabled us to go to city council and justify lifting the caps because individual drivers could oppose it.

LI: What can research bring to organizing?

PZ: When the Employee Rights Center started in 1999, we wanted to do employee rights training with nonprofit social service agencies. So, we did a study of one of those agencies. We found out by the end of it that for the workers of these organizations, it would be great, but the managers of the nonprofits were uptight about it. We figured the reason they were uptight about it was because they were all nonunion. They didn't want workers' rights training or knowledge as a part of their work. That was the first time we reached out to the contacts we had in the Department of Communication at UCSD to help us with this type of work. The important part is that we knew what we wanted, similar to the taxi workers' research. We knew we didn't have the capacity for what we wanted so we found researchers to answer the questions we had already posed.

It was easier for us to build relationships because we had experience and CPI was well known in the labor movement. It had credibility because of the studies they did that related to what people in unions wanted to know and addressed what their issues were. They had built those connections in academia and unions as well as trust. Connections are crucial. How you make them is the art of organizing. In order to have those relationships you've got to build trust.

MH: If you have that kind of trust with researchers and they know what they want, working together will be easy. When you have this, researchers and students want to continue help- ing even if they've finished the projects they've been working on. With "Driven to Despair," we found that as long as we're actually trying to change policy, and the researchers deliver what they've said they'll deliver, this kind of work is amazing for the labor movement. But researchers need to know what their research is and who the community they're researching is. The drivers need to trust them. Trust is important.

LI: Are there other pitfalls, other than trust, that you've come across when working with researchers?

PZ: Another issue can be overpromising. You need to have a good understanding of what deliverables are possible. Having a clear idea of what you're doing, what you're bringing, and what the expectations are is necessary. Academics need to be honest about that, recognize it's something that can be negotiated, and recognize there's equal power between them and the community they're working with.

LI: Can you elaborate on what you mean by recognizing power in these relationships?

PZ: There are power dynamics that come up that can hurt either side. People have to understand them and recognize that how you deal with them can be problematic. There will always be power—knowledge is power—and academics have to be comfortable with the fact that this dynamic will exist. You must learn who people are within the community, what's happening within it, and how to navigate it. Once you enter the organizing world you become a part of this; you can't deny or ignore these things because you're an academic. If an academic is going to get involved in organizing, they've got to learn how to play and get to know the turf. If you don't know, you find people who can help guide you through that process because it is always there. You can't escape it. You have to learn it.

LI: How can researchers be accountable to the workers in the organizations they collaborate with?

PZ: It comes down to power. That's why academics have to negotiate on deliverables and expectations. Negotiations need to happen up front about who's doing what so there's a common understanding among everyone. That's how you become accountable. During these negotiations, if you're realistic, then it'll be a positive experience. If you're not, you need to recognize that the other side has power too. It's a two-way relationship. You need to be ready to negotiate and address expectations.

MH: Negotiating, accountability, and not overpromising things is important. I also don't like framing these relationships as "I scratch your back, you scratch mine." If someone wants to do something because they're passionate about it, because you feel like you'll add value, then you should do it. I'll always remember these kinds of people. But people must be accountable for the things they say they'll do.

LI: Is there anything different about organizing for worker power in the context of platforms like Uber and Lyft or are the same strategies being carried forward?

PZ: When a new technology is introduced, there's this idea that the technology supersedes all of these human elements. But I think what's important to remember is that the human element, the question of power, still comes through. It just occurs through a different form.

MH: I think there's three kinds of organizing—three people, three roles. One is people who are with you all the time. You always have to keep those people close. Then there are people who need you to talk to them, they listen to you, they may be working directly with you and helping with the organizing you're doing. Lastly, there are people who will never be satisfied with you no matter what you're doing. Although you want to spend a lot of time attracting these people because they are influential amongst other workers, don't waste your time. Do talk to these people when you get the chance but don't put too much pressure on yourself to get them to listen to you. Some people cannot differentiate between questions of ownership and doing something for the goodwill of everybody.

One of my best models for outreach is that I always make sure there are ways for me to communicate with the people who are with me from the get-go, who know the work I'm doing. I always make sure I invite them to meetings. I also try to reach the individuals we are advocating for and show them what we are doing for them on their behalf while they're not participating. That's the organizing piece I've been using over the last fourteen years.

The second thing to be aware of is that you're changing people's lives. People come to our office with issues that aren't directly about work, like issues with immigration. People come here for different reasons and for different resources because we are a trusted organization.

With the driving platforms, we need to change. No matter what. If we don't adapt to these innovations we're already too late in the game. Uber and Lyft came in a long time ago and promised us $35–$40 per hour. They never delivered that, but they did take the industry from us. These platforms are competing amongst themselves too, but they are winning the game.

I had a friend who bought a car and told me she wanted to start driving for Uber or Lyft. I didn't tell her to not do it, even though I think she can do better things with her life, but I did tell her to do two things. First, I told her to put her mileage down and check how much she's making and how many miles she's driving. Compare those numbers. Drive for a week for them and then come back to me. After she came back, she realized she was making $2.10. Less than $2.50 per hour. Through practice, I was able to show her what she was missing.

We want to show and tell the drivers to forget about Uber and Lyft. What's stopping us from changing the industry? We know how to innovate. We developed our own app called Ride United.

When it comes to outreach, most of the time I'm not asking people to come to our union or to join us. I'm asking what's preventing them from making money because of this technology [Uber]. Tell me. But you need to listen. Listening is key to organizing. At the beginning, organizers should say, "I'm here to say hi. I want to know you, what your situation is, how business is going, and if there's anything you want to tell me. I may have some ideas to help you!" That's an icebreaker.

But this period is a tech period. We cannot go back. We have to do these innovations. This is something we talked about in 2014 when these apps were being introduced. We said we needed to focus on three areas: innovation, customer service, and price reduction. When it comes to Uber and Lyft, I'm not worried about what they do and the way they do it. They're successful because the technology is there and customers like it, so if we use similar technologies then at least we are competing with them. We need the technology, though. MTS has even been talking about getting rid of the meter system by next year, so we need to move on with this technology.

PZ: We knew we wanted an app—but the fact that there's very few in the United States and in the taxi industry sort of lets you know that it's going to be hard. There must be some objective barriers.[3]

I mean, if we had a lot of money and we were doing marketing research, if somebody had venture capital, they might say, "Okay, we're going to go for resources," and then they would say, "We're going to go here, and here, and here, and here." But we didn't have that.

Having a Tech Workers Coalition was very important for UTWSD. We would have no way of knowing you at UCSD. I don't know how else we would've met. We were just living in different worlds. Having a tech platform for human connections with people with know-how and common values can help make things work.

RK UPADHYA

TECH WORKERS COALITION (BAY AREA)

In conversation with Tamara Kneese

RK Upadhya is an electrical engineer currently working in Texas. He is a member of the Democratic Socialists of America (DSA) and its Communist Caucus. RK was part of the early wave of Tech Workers Coalition (TWC) organizing in the San Francisco Bay Area from 2016 to 2019 and has long connected Marxist organizing histories to contemporary struggles. For instance, in articles for *Notes from Below*, *Science for the People*, and *Logic Magazine*.

Tamara Kneese first met RK at TWC meetings around the Bay Area, then spent more time with RK and fellow TWC organizers Paige Panter and Sterling Radcliffe at Log Out! Resistance Within and Against Platform Labour, a symposium organized by a McLuhan Centre for Culture and Technology working group at the University of Toronto in March 2018. Log Out! focused on resistance and labor organizing in the digital economy and connecting workers and researchers, including several future Capacitor Collective members and other contributors to this book.[1] Tamara has invited members of TWC to speak to her college classes at the University of San Francisco and participated in TWC learning clubs and other events, becoming a core organizer for the TWC Teach-In event in fall 2023, when she pivoted to a full-time role in the tech industry.

Tech Workers Coalition is a democratically structured, all-volunteer, worker-led organization that builds tech worker power through rank-and-file self-education and education initiatives. TWC was established in the San Francisco Bay Area in 2014 by Rachel Melendes, a cafeteria worker and labor organizer, and Matt Schaefer, a software engineer. In its early days, the group focused on how to get the tech industry's white-collar workers to actually think of themselves as workers, and importantly, as workers building power alongside more precarious workers in and around the tech industry. To build coalitions and cross-collar solidarity. Early TWC campaigns supported hotel workers in Santa Clara, connecting subcontracted workers on tech campuses to full-time office workers. During the first Trump administration, TWC organized with tech workers against Palantir's contributions to a mass deportation database.

TWC is a horizontal organization and has chapters in several US cities and in other cities around the world. Because of its decentralized nature, membership tends to ebb and flow, and many activities happen in local chapters around specific issue campaigns or online, via Slack or webinars that provide networked spaces for information sharing. The next several conversations feature TWC members from different chapters, occupations, and periods of time, a testament to the multifaceted composition of the organization.

This conversation took place in June 2024, prior to Trump's reelection.

Tamara Kneese: Let's start with how you became involved with organizing, and with TWC, and some of the context around the early years.

RK Upadhya: That was back in 2016. I was working at a wastewater plant as a controls engineer. At that point I had been doing engineering stuff in the energy and resources sector for a long time. I wasn't doing much organizing back then. I had been involved with college campus environmental activism and socialist book clubs and stuff, but nothing after graduating. I was just kind of chilling, reading and writing, and reflecting about the engineering profession and technology through a Marxist lens—like, are engineers workers or are they something else? What's the nature of the professional-managerial class (PMC)? Blah blah blah.

Around that time, I joined the Industrial Workers of the World (IWW) to get more involved in actual organizing. When I joined, one of the IWW guys was like, "Hey, you're like an engineer, right? Well, we had some tech workers over in San Francisco reach out to us, and they had some kind of group. Maybe you'd be interested." So, I checked it out and that was TWC. The US presidential election had just happened [where Trump was elected]. By December 2016, lots of people were looking to get involved, and the TWC general meetings were getting quite big.

TK: TWC, in a lot of ways, originated as this way of providing an opportunity for cross-collar solidarity, in terms of supporting service workers on tech campuses. I'm curious what the conversations were like around engaging with gig workers or TVCs [Temps, Vendors, and Contractors] within large companies like Google?

RKU: There's an interesting roller coaster ride around that. TWC was started as a kind of a front group for UNITE HERE.[2] I think it was the president of the San Francisco local and this software engineer named Matt, they were neighbors and they got to talking in 2014 or so, and said, "Hey, it'd be great if we can get more white-collar tech workers to help support some of these union campaigns among the service workers at these 'Big Tech' campuses." And that was the start of Tech Workers Coalition. The idea was to invoke the traditional image of the techie to be in favor of these union campaigns. In 2016 and 2017, we didn't stop doing that, but the major shift was our focus toward stuff around the Trump election, and the ethics of technology and what it means to be a technical worker working on technologies that might be used for things like ethnic cleansing and deportations and all that nefarious stuff. At the same time, there were still ongoing union campaigns, and whenever there was an ask for support, we would mobilize.

It was mid-2017 when all that got submerged into a broader and more radical vision of worker power and workplace organizing. That's when we started talking more seriously about making TWC a worker-organizing project. We began focusing on the question of how to get technical, white-collar workers to actually think of themselves as workers and identify more closely with the service workers who are fighting union campaigns, the people of UNITE HERE, and so on. Then, how do we substantively connect this identity back into resisting imperialism and undermine the use of technology being deployed for nefarious ends?

TK: Were there any tensions that emerged between workers of different classes, or at different parts of the value chain?

RKU: In 2017, we were focused on this question of worker identity and the question of cross-occupation worker identity. That's when we came up with our major slogans, like "Worker Power in the Tech Industry" and "If You Work in the Tech Industry, You Are a Worker." We don't care about the specific occupation; we don't care if you're a software engineer or a contractor or a janitor or whoever. We want this to be for everybody. We want to create a cross-occupation identity and all fight for each other's interests.

Still, there were plenty of discussions and debates about how to actually go about all this. In retrospect, I think there was an open question—especially for me personally—about what this cross-occupation solidarity and identity should look like. It's one thing to say that this is a project for all workers, but why would a cafeteria worker, for example, join TWC and not just UNITE HERE? What does it mean to be a cross-occupation space?

There were some other hangups around this question of identity. How do we deal with class guilt? There was a habit of people in the larger tech movement to whip themselves about being white-collar workers and would outright deny that they were "real" workers.

On the flip side, there was a tendency to erase any differences whatsoever between occupations, and say you're the same kind of worker whether you're making $35,000 and commuting in from Stockton or if you're a full-time Google worker making $300,000 a year. Well, that's nonsense, of course there's differences there. These people experience capitalism very differently and have a different association with the supply chain. That's important to recognize, not just for personal reasons but for strategic reasons. So, there were a lot of conversations around these different kinds of attitudes around class and identity that we were trying to work through.

TK: I'm curious how people within TWC were thinking about their relationship to knowledge production at that time and how you think about it now. Have things shifted in terms of what you think works well in an organizing context? You've also written a lot about workers' inquiry as a technique, and how workers' inquiry can become a mechanism for expanding how workers can engage in knowledge production, and their own capacity for it, outside of the university.

RKU: Yeah, I think a lot of us were history nerds or Marxist nerds or whatever. I was trying to theorize this stuff before I even got involved in organizing, so I was very happy to try to merge theory and practice within TWC. Our thinking was: let's study from previous rounds of struggle, with an emphasis on struggles in and around technology and science, on autonomous worker organizing, etc. A lot of this was driven by people's personal interests, and I personally had an interest in workers' inquiry and this idea that we should be conducting surveys and interviews and inquiries, and just get people to talk, and then, to talk collectively about who they were and what their experiences were like.

We had the more traditional reading groups, of course. Like, let's read this piece about the janitors' strike in Silicon Valley back in the '90s or this other text about struggles by IBM workers. I think reading history is great because it puts you into this historical lineage and you feel like you have these political ancestors, these antecedents of what you're doing that you can draw inspiration from and see yourself as part of a deeper legacy. Then there are takeaway lessons—what did they do right, what did they do wrong, what were the questions they were asking and strategic planning they were doing, and then we try to apply all that to a modern context.

On the topic of workers' inquiry, I was coming into all this from a more theoretical perspective, from reading stuff about workers' inquiry in places like *Viewpoint Magazine* and the like. I thought: okay, I like the framework, I like the historical lineage, but at what point does the workers' inquiry method just become a way to facilitate a good meeting and do basic onboarding? A lot of our so-called workers' inquiry was simply an introductory meeting to TWC, to get together a group of tech workers, a mix of experienced organizers with newer folks. The new folks, they're curious, they're mad, they want to organize their workplace, they want to learn more about what's happening. We would just walk through who we all were. We'd discuss: where do you work, what kind of problems are you facing? How long have you been in the industry? Do you want to stay in tech? What are your coworkers like, what kind of stuff do you work on, etc. So in this context, it's like an extended icebreaker, an extended introduction. It's all just workers "inquiring" with each other.

TK: How would you differentiate workers' inquiry from other kinds of organizing meetings?

RKU: Now, on top of the basic introductory discussions, I suppose there were useful practical aspects that maybe distinguish it from really basic meeting facilitation. A couple of points on this.

Number one: a lot of people were coming into the movement from a very high level within the tech industry, thinking about high-level political abstractions. For example, they come in aghast about Trump, they want to know what to do about Trump. We were really trying to ground these general concerns into their own personal day-to-day life and what their actual experiences were. I think it was a real useful way to bring them down from those high-level political abstractions where there's no clear answers about what to do, or from online discussions and debates about theory and politics, or the news cycles covering the outrage of the day. To bring them back into their own life and their own experiences and working conditions, what's actually happening around them and with the people they're around. I think it was useful as an organizing tool and as a framing device: okay, there's all this stuff that's motivating us, but what is within our reach? And how do we use that as the building block to build a larger radical project?

The second point: the usefulness of having these conversations about *each others'* experiences and sharing what we're going through and what frustrates us about the industry. Why we're unsatisfied and why we're restive. I think this is common across a lot of workers' inquiry, but people can very easily normalize what they experience and think: "Okay, well, this is happening; this sucks, but this is natural, it's normal." I think hearing other people say they have the same complaints can denormalize that a little bit, and especially if we build an organizing space where we're not saying anything is normal, we're always saying, "Yeah, that sucks, we should fight it." It's about politicizing what people may otherwise consider to be "normal" problems, and saying, "Actually no, we can think about fighting this." It's about universalizing what may be perceived as individual problems.

Those are two specific things the workers' inquiry framework was doing. One more thing to mention, around more rigorous knowledge production: there were a few people very interested in trying to do more intensive investigations and actually learn something about techno-capitalism, from talking in-depth about what people were doing, where they were in the workplace, where they were in the supply chain, what kind of software they were using, what were their teams and what do their teams interface with, stuff like that. But I think that we didn't really go very far. We would need actual experts in political economy, experts in the corporate structures of Silicon Valley, and all that to facilitate that sort of discussion, to know what kind of questions to ask and how to draw conclusions.

TK: It feels like we're in a moment right now where there's a resurgence of tech worker organizing, but it does feel a little bit different than the early wave of anti-Trump protests. What does your conjunctural analysis look like for how the general situation has changed for the tech workers movement since 2017?[3]

RKU: Right now, it does feel like an echo, or a repeat, of the Trump moment. There is mobilization around similar things, like the role of tech companies in facilitating imperialism.

One big difference is that back then, there was a real novelty to the idea that tech workers were going to protest their own companies. One of the early actions in 2017 was a protest against Palantir [data analytics company cofounded by Peter Thiel]. I think there were maybe like twenty, twenty-five people there, but it still made national news, just because of the novelty. We had a lot of discussions about this, that we have a lot of media power for some dumb reason, so let's exploit it, but let's also make sure we don't just become a media organization. This sort of thing is no longer surprising. In fact, I think it's much harder for actions by tech workers to really make the news that much anymore. Actions like the Google sit-in will make the news, but it's no longer this shocking action that captures headlines and provokes wider public discussion.

Another difference today is that companies are prepared for all this. They've faced about eight years of worker mobilizations now, and like with the crackdown at Google, they've more or less shed their pretension to be progressive, open, or even democratic companies. They will fire a bunch of people if they step out of line, unlike back then, when it did feel like there was a lot you could get away with. Google was even straight-up hiring people with union backgrounds who would talk about that during interviews! I don't think that would happen now, but before 2020, it just wasn't something that managers were thinking of as an issue at all.

Another major thing that has changed is the economic situation. The 2016–2020 period was characterized by massive growth in the tech industry, facilitated by zero-percent interest rates. That's kind of burst. Now we're seeing layoffs and contractions in the tech industry, and I do think this can undermine potential labor power and the confidence of workers to mobilize. On the other hand, maybe increasing precarity will lead to more identification with the identity of the "worker" and more desire for unions. Anyways, that's my brief conjunctural analysis.

TK: To shift topics—there's more back-and-forth movement now than I've ever seen between academic institutions, policy circles, and tech. But I think that the idea that academics are helping tech workers and platform workers organize, as scholars, is not quite the right framing. How do you think about the relationship between scholarly work and organizing?

RKU: I remember at the Log Out! conference, I had a lot of fun asking people whether they were organizing their workplaces at their universities. Because surely academic scholars can't just be talking about gig workers and tech workers—they also have to see themselves as workers, right? And that's also where workers' inquiry can be interesting, you can bring in observers and say, so what about you? What are you up to, what's your working conditions like? Are you also organizing? And that can get them to recognize that, oh I'm not actually just a researcher or writer or whatever, I'm a worker too.

There was a great experience with this in the early days of post-2016 TWC. At that time, we were getting a lot of journalists' attention. So, we'd have people from BuzzFeed or *The New York Times* or wherever sometimes show up to events and talk to people. It was the first workers' inquiry event I tried to do, I think in early 2017, and we had maybe like ten, fifteen tech workers going through a worksheet, talking to each other in groups of two to three about our workplace experiences. There was a BuzzFeed News journalist who was there on the beat, and I welcomed her to join us, but told her she would also have talk about her own workplace experiences. So, she joined the conversation, and she ended up talking with us as a worker about workplace organizing. She kept coming back to other events, and it was funny because on one hand, she's trying to write stories about tech worker organizing, but she was also talking about her own workplace, brainstorming organizing tactics, swapping advice. I believe she ended up going on to help start the BuzzFeed News Union.

I think that's a great example of what it looks like to break down the barriers between industry and academia, or journalism, or whatever. It's not about professors bestowing knowledge upon people. It's about seeing a university, and journalism, as part of the supply chain. Strategically, it was very advantageous for us to have journalists who were part of the movement, who would basically just write borderline propaganda for us and about us.

Back to academia. Now, I'm saying this as someone who enjoys reading academic work, but I'm not sure who reads anymore. Relative to ten years ago I don't really read that much anymore. We're all watching TikTok dances or whatever. Point being, if academic workers are researching tech workers or gig workers, and then they put that into a nice paper or book or whatever, well, that can't be it, because I don't think any of the tech workers or gig workers are necessarily going to read that.

TK: Are there any more recent examples that come to mind?

RKU: Recently I was looking at a fairly famous community organization called DRUM—Desis Rising Up and Moving.

It's a strong base-building organization in New York City that organizes working-class South Asians, like a lot of Bengali taxi drivers. If you look on their website, they have an explicit message that says: "I'm sorry, but we do not have capacity to help academic researchers and students with their inquiries." I think that's interesting because it shows that it's too easy for this stuff to be a one-way street, where a certain brand of academics might insist that they're helping the movement but really it's about writing their own thing, and no one in the movement is ever gonna see it. It's purely for the researcher's own peers and their own career.

It comes back to the question of what are we actually doing with knowledge? I think today, with information glut and whatnot, first we have to figure out ways to erase the dividing lines between academia and the subject of academia, organizers and activists and scholars and writers, and create a more consistent loop of knowledge and practice. If people who mainly work in academia are processing this knowledge, how do we make sure it's brought back to workers in a useful form and in ways which inform their practices? That could be as simple as having a circuit of academics doing political education sessions with people or something. That's a really simple idea that comes to mind. And then secondly, seeing academia as a site of struggle. Not just accepting the current terms of what academia is, but to fight to institutionally transform academia into something that backs people's movements and working-class struggles.

TK: This raises the question of how to think about the tech workers movement in the context of broader social movements. What is the importance of the "tech worker" for, say, struggles against unethical tech? What are the lessons that we can take from the things that people were trying to do during the early days of TWC?

RKU: There is a usefulness to emphasizing a specific type of worker and strategically organizing around that, drawing on the classical kind of Marxist formulation about who are the people that can leverage the most at particular points in the supply chain. The idea being that a tech workers' movement can build power in the tech industry so that we can disrupt and take over or shut down key nodes. Also, that the workers in these areas are arguably best positioned to understand and carry out this stuff. Of course, this is debatable, but there's still an important place for the classical Marxist framework of looking at who has the direct power in a certain part of the supply chain, the power and means to act if they are organized.

There's a very vulgar version of that, which says we can't criticize any worker anywhere, because we need to win that person over to the cause, in order to end or reform that specific industry. At a certain point it just becomes ridiculous—like, we gotta also unionize the fucking guards at Auschwitz? Give me a fucking break, we can just shoot them. Who cares!—and that does apply to some parts of tech work. Some things we don't need to worry about appropriating or reforming, we just need to shut it down through mass action or state power or something. That goes back to questions of knowledge production, information and higher-level theory, to understand what do we actually want to keep for a progressive future, a socialist future or whatever, and what parts can we toss into trash.

Also, how are workers themselves thinking about this? In TWC, there were people who came in and they're nodding their heads at the socialists and anarchists yapping about capitalism and worker power. Then afterward, we're chit-chatting and I'd say something like, "Damn, ads and ad-tech, those are pretty bad, huh? Wouldn't it be great to get rid of ads?" And they'd be like, "Oh, well you know that's how we get our money. So they're not that bad." Clearly, we had a bit more work to do there!

This raises a bigger question: what does it take to radicalize tech workers? Or workers in any particular area? This goes back to the stuff I was studying before I joined TWC, about the 1960s and '70s in Europe and the US, when theorization about PMCs was emerging. In Europe, there was a lot of really in-depth analysis and discussions by Marxists and by communists who were trying to understand all these new techno-scientific workers that were emerging in the postwar industries, and they're trying to grapple with the questions of whether these people were proper proletarians or were they petit bourgeois, and were they down with socialism? There was real study into what was happening sociologically and economically with old-school "tech workers."

TK: What theories from that historical and political era do you find especially salient for understanding the positionality of tech workers in the contemporary context?

RKU: I think the most convincing analysis I saw from that era was from Greek-French Marxist theorist Nicos Poulantzas, who argued that these middle classes—which is how I would categorize most techno-scientific workers today—overall tend to be very squishy. They will go along with the majority, whatever the most aggressive classes in society are going for. When capitalists are doing well and things are looking okay, they'll go with them. When there's a mass proletarian movement, they'll shift their allegiances to that. They are rather opportunistic.

I've had this discussion with other ex-TWC comrades, about the actual potential of a tech workers' movement, broadly speaking. Our conclusion was that it depends on what's actually happening amongst the much wider strata of working-class people. Because if there's nothing happening, then there's not going to be much going on in the tech workers movement.

On the other hand, if there's a very vibrant mass movement, then that will be the conditions that will drive the radicalization of the tech workers movement as well. What that means for would-be tech organizers, I'm not sure; obviously you don't just wait around. I would say, do what you can, connect tech workers as much as possible to other movements and organizations. Keep plugging away where you're at, lay seeds that will sprout in more revolutionary times.

I hope the organizing we did in early TWC days helped lay the seeds for the more expansive activity that we're seeing now.

TK: I feel like that's a good place to end!

ERIK H
TECH WORKERS COALITION
(SEATTLE)
In conversation with Tamara Kneese

Erik H is an organizer and member of Seattle's Tech Workers Coalition, a chapter of the independent affinity group that facilitates cross-collar organizing in the tech industry. Erik is a cafeteria worker at the University of Washington (UW) and a member of Local 1488 of the Washington Federation of State Employees (WFSE). His various jobs and organizing experiences embody the cross-collar organizing work of Tech Workers Coalition members.

Erik started his career as an operations engineer and later took a job washing dishes at a major tech company's campus. He has also worked as an organizer, union rep, and food service worker on a university campus. Having grown up, lived, and worked in the South Bay, Erik was one of the organizers behind South Bay Mutual Aid, which provided assistance to people in San Jose during the early days of the COVID-19 pandemic, which he discussed in the *TWC Newsletter* as "abolitionist cybernetics" that combines systems theory and principles of mutual aid to organize tech worker struggles.

Tamara Kneese spoke with Erik for this contribution, which is how they first connected.[1] During the early pandemic, when it wasn't feasible to hold in-person meetings in TWC hubs, the TWC Slack and the *TWC Newsletter* became spaces where workers could connect across geographic regions. Erik and Tamara met several times over Zoom to prepare the *Newsletter* entry and continued to communicate about organizing in the Bay Area and Seattle. Erik and Tamara also started working on a second *Newsletter* piece that addressed the food-delivery platform that the University of Washington implemented, engaging some UW students in a critique of a system that turned university food service workers into platform delivery workers without their consent. That piece is still unfinished.

Tamara Kneese: Tell us about your first encounter with labor organizing.

Erik H: There was a graduate workers' strike at UC Santa Cruz while I was there. They had a picket down at this entrance at the bottom of a hill which wasn't near anything, but they'd have rallies there. When you would go up to where the classrooms and cafeteria buildings were, everything was pretty much happening "as is." Other than the grad students not working everything else was happening. Dining halls were open; they were being cleaned and maintained. If the dining workers were on strike, I think that would be more disruptive and potentially create an opportunity for more divisiveness. I wasn't into organizing at that time, but the grad workers strike didn't affect me in any way. When workers go on strike who do things you rely on, you're going to notice it.

TK: You went on to work in the kitchens of Google, on a major tech campus. What was it like there?

EH: What I saw in the tech campus, the support work, cooking, cleaning, that kind of stuff, was made invisible. The janitors, for example, they work at nighttime. There's a temporal way of segregating work. With the food service, we had our own entrance. The kitchens were in the back and kept separate and walled off. There were physical barriers to keep people from seeing into a lot of the kitchen. At Google, they have a lot of these kitchenettes on every floor of their office. They have coolers that are kept fully stocked with various drinks and snacks and whatnot that have to be at the front of the fridge for aesthetic purposes. You can't fill those overnight—it's a constant process of refilling the snack fridge and making sure everything is neatly lined up within it. Although these workers are in the same physical space as the ones doing the coding they aren't really acknowledged. People don't pay attention to them. There's a huge class component to this. The support staff make up about half the workforce there, but you wouldn't know that because these workers are made invisible except when it is impossible to do so because they have to be in the same physical space. Even when these workers are there it's still as if they aren't.

TK: Did you see common patterns in the two industries now that you work at a university again? How does solidarity happen if workers remain siloed?

EH: Solidarity does exist, but workers are siloed here too. In terms of organizing at Google, we had this campaign at the Googleplex, the main campus in Mountain View, California as well as San Francisco and Seattle, where all the food service workers became organized. Things were picking up in Atlanta and New York too. This campaign was a part of a bigger push. UNITE HERE was organizing the food service workers but were not involved in any kind of tech organizing or with the people organizing tech. Engineers were starting to organize at the same time, and we discovered that the roots of both struggles overlap a lot. In theory, if everyone could be in communication with one another and coordinate together, we could be incredibly powerful.

Service workers at the University of Washington have been talking about how they're trying to connect with UAW [United Auto Workers], the union for grad student workers at the university. We were able to coordinate with them a few years ago [at Google] when we were in similar strike positions. Here, SEIU [Service Employees International Union] represents mostly librarians, not service workers. Service workers like me—the dining hall, janitorial, and maintenance staff—are represented by WFSE, the Washington State Federation of Employees. AFSCME [American Federation of State, County, and Municipal Employees] is the umbrella union. So, we're segregated from that broader organizing that's happening but we're also not supposed to be doing any organizing independently.

TK: My friend, Zach Schwartz-Weinstein, wrote about the coalitions that formed at Yale from the 1960s to the 1980s. There were different strikes which included cafeteria workers, clerical workers, students, and at some points adjunct faculty. It was about building spaces of solidarity across various sectors of the university and across race, class, and gender. But things eventually fell apart.

EH: I think there's potential to be very effective in organizing in coalitions, both in terms of getting people what they want (i.e., whatever they're striking for) but also building those connections between the academic and service worlds. The tech campus could be a space to do that. Yes, the campus is focused on the academic and it has labor to support that, but that labor isn't really a part of the campus in the same way.

It's similar at Google. We have kitchen workers, but they aren't considered a part of the Google workforce. There's also this historical presumption that if they were to go on strike or complain they could just be replaced by hiring new people. When I was a part of the bargaining team for the recent WFSE contract negotiation, the employer's representatives said, "If you go on strike, your job isn't protected." People know it's not true. They can't fire us. They could potentially fire one or two people but they can't fire all of us. If they could hire additional staff, they'd already be doing it, because we're understaffed as it is. Everybody knows it. But this pressure point isn't used, in an organizing sense, or it's not made clear that these threats are just off the table. Yet, both the school and the union were saying our jobs could potentially be at risk if we did a workplace action.

TK: As somebody who's worked in both contexts, tech and academia, what do you think the role of research is right now? Is there a way that academics can be useful? Or is it another form of extraction and looking for new field sites?

EH: I think academic research has value and serves a purpose, but who are their questions directed at/to? Are they being directed to academia itself? Are they being directed toward the union leadership? Are they being directed toward the actual union rank-and-file themselves? I work with a lot of students and they're asking, "What can we do to support you all?" And really, it's a lot of listening that's needed, because again, this is a class issue. But people are often ignored rather than treated as equals. These workers need to be treated as authorities about their workplace, their lives, and themselves.

TK: Often, academics who research rideshare drivers or other forms of gig work seem to focus on the immiseration of workers. I'm increasingly turned off by this particular kind of research. Have you had any experiences with people turning you into a research subject? Or have you had encounters with researchers in this context?

EH: Those feelings are kind of mutual. My way of dealing with it is by not engaging with or hiding away from the more academic side of things. There have been a lot of state campaigns, various organizing campaigns on tech campuses, or campaigns around specific issues, like on Project Nimbus or customs and border protection. What these campaigns had in common is that they made demands on their employer. Sometimes the employer will throw them a bone here and there but most of these campaigns haven't succeeded. I'm not saying people shouldn't be doing these kinds of campaigns. I appreciate people doing the right thing even if they know it's not going to succeed because it's the right thing to do. But there should be more honest and sober reflection on how they work and how or why they failed. The issue isn't what they were pursuing, but more so questioning how they went about trying to succeed or achieve their objectives in regard to what they were pursuing.

As I mentioned earlier, UAW has working groups, they have a lot going on. People in my field don't necessarily have the capacity to do that kind of work—to join working groups—because they're working multiple jobs. I've never been a fan of electoralism or voting to decide on things, but I recognize that given we have a bad contract right now, and in the absence of systems set up for direct action, voting is, to a lot of people, the only voice they feel they have. I think we need to take the approach of asking, "how do you take what people are saying, what their needs are, and supporting that from whatever position you're in?"

TK: When I was a professor at the University of San Francisco, a private Jesuit liberal arts school, during the pandemic, it was made very clear that faculty, even tenure-track faculty, were expendable. It shook some people out of their belief that they weren't workers. I was delighted to see that my data science colleagues were attending union meetings and wanted to organize. But even people who research labor often don't fully view themselves as workers. I wonder if it's related to the old, pretend objectivity of social science research, where, in order to study something, you must view yourself as being removed from it?

EH: It does sound like that probably does have a lot to do with it. But it's also important to recognize that different workers on campus, including tech workers and campus support staff, live in different worlds in many respects. So, you get this situation where there isn't much support, not because you look down on something or don't value it, but because you don't think about it. One way to develop a good understanding of how people are doing is by saying, "These jobs are available. You can take them. You will get firsthand experience of both what they do and how they're perceived by the people they're working for."

TK: A lot of grad students take jobs, for example, as Uber drivers for a few months and then write about it. I knew someone in college who came from a wealthy family. For his thesis, he worked at Walmart and wrote about it. This is a great example of someone trying out a class position for a little bit, using it as fodder for your own research, but then returning to your own safe position in a different class.

EH: I think about this in terms of what people need or would give them a good quality of life. In terms of when I was in tech versus doing this, I can confidently say, what would make people working these kinds of service positions have a good quality of life is probably a $100,000 salary. When it comes down to it, there's a lot of stuff about respect and how these workers are viewed but ultimately those attitudes play out in our system as pay.

TK: It really is about material conditions. Having enough money to pay the rent and to afford the things that make for a good life, would make a much bigger difference than a change in perspective. What we're talking about is the need for real structural transformation.

EH: If more people had that perspective, then they would recognize that taking a working-class job and then going back to their other job and writing about their experiences, while that can be good for understanding the position of these workers, at the same time, these workers are still there after you've left. They're still doing the work. They still worry about money.

TK: Recognizing the limits of what research can do is important, but I have been interested in the ways specific kinds of research can be a part of organizing. Especially thinking back to Occupy Wall Street, where there was an interesting focus on creating texts that could radicalize a more general audience. There were a lot of public lectures at Occupy and the People's University which tried to make space for radical ideas. What do you think of public intellectual work that isn't necessarily about turning workers themselves into a research experiment?

EH: There's the whole process of culture, how it's created, and how it feeds back into itself and how things like labor are viewed. I'd say you have people who are more interested in these things academically and those who are participating in them. But, going back to the people at the bottom-end of this hierarchy, like the food service workers at Google or at the university, if they did labor actions, how is that going to be viewed by academics? The point with these actions is to be disruptive. People are going to be disrupted. Is this going to build solidarity between the two groups or will it do the opposite? Does it build solidarity between some workers and not others?

Also, you are talking about how academics being removed from, or being neutral about certain things, can lead to them having a different perspective if they're not in that space directly. I don't think that's just an academic issue. The people who work in the union office, they're disconnected in the same way. They don't know what's going on because they don't live it. I think the issue is less about having certain politics and more about how you live and what social circles you run in.

TK: It's important to talk about the long-term relationship between rank-and-file workers and unions, because sometimes the goal is to simply plant the flag and say, "We have a union!" But the idea that getting the union is the end goal of the struggle is incorrect. You have to continuously put work into the union. The union is you—you are the union.

EH: It is. You can have whatever structure you want, but that structure is only as good as how well it represents the will of the people within it. I'll keep you posted, but the union just sent out their "you vote online" link, which a lot of people have problems with. It wasn't translated into Spanish or Tagalog, which are the primary languages spoken by the vast majority of kitchen and janitorial workers at UW, so they are left out completely. It seemed very targeted. There are a bunch of people who are ready to walk out should the vote not pass. It will be interesting to see how things play out both if there's a walkout during a busy time at school but also how the union may intervene. The union will be given a choice whether to stop what's happening or try to co-opt it because there aren't many options other than that.[2]

KATE SIM
NO TECH FOR APARTHEID
In conversation with Tamara Kneese

Kate Sim has a background as an anti-sexual violence organizer and later worked as a policy advisor at Google, where she specialized in child safety issues. While at Google, she became an organizer with No Tech for Apartheid, an international campaign focused on ending cloud computing military contracts between Google, Amazon, and Israel—including "Project Nimbus," Google's cloud computing contract with the Israeli military. Kate is also an academic researcher, and someone whose understanding of the relationship between knowledge production and praxis has led to a new role as the principal on a three-year research project focused on Children's Online Safety and Privacy Research (COSPR) with the University of Western Australia's Tech and Policy Lab.

In 2023, Tamara Kneese and Kate were introduced by a mutual friend who is also involved with Tech Workers Coalition and No Tech for Apartheid. Tamara and Kate also both attended the October 2024 Circuit Breakers Conference in San Francisco, co-organized by Tech Workers Coalition and Collective Action in Tech. Tamara spoke with Kate two days before she was fired from her job at Google, along with forty-nine other employees, as part of the company's retaliation against an April 2024 "day of action" organized by No Tech for Apartheid that included sit-ins at high-profile Google offices.

Tamara Kneese: Can you tell us about yourself, how you ended up working at Google, and how you got involved with organizing?

Kate Sim: For most of my life I've considered myself an organizer. In college, around 2012–2013, I started organizing against sexual violence, particularly around victims' rights in the context of social media and online gaming in the United States. We were a younger generation, and when Gamergate was happening a lot of women with histories of sexual violence were leveraging social media to find each other. I met up with five other survivors, students, organizers, and working together, we led a national-level campaign for legal reform. That was my first foray into local—at a campus level—and national-level organizing. After that, I worked for a year at a rape crisis center in Seoul. I grew up in Korea until I was eleven, so it was interesting to go back as an adult and a diasporic person and continue that work. Through that organizing, I was starting to see ways in which feminist and gender-forward spaces didn't quite know how to make sense of technology, especially around tech-facilitated gender-based violence, both online and offline.

As I was delving more into the tech world as well as understanding gender and the relational dynamics of power, I ended up at the Oxford Internet Institute for my master's degree, doing my thesis project on the ways childcare social services were using predictive risk scoring to identify people who are likely to experience or commit child abuse. That was my first foray into "responsible AI," although I don't think that phrase had taken off yet in 2015.

I enjoyed doing ethnographic work, especially talking to social workers about this tension between evidence-based and numerical forms of knowledge versus their gut feelings. As people who've been working in social care for ten-plus years, how do those two different forms of knowledge production come up against each other, in this moment of austerity, as childcare services are being cut drastically and law enforcement is increasingly the modus operandi for how these social and public services operate? At the same time, I did a bunch of side projects around feminized personal safety, tech solutionism, and cyberfeminist theoretical frameworks. We leaned into ideas about design and encoding assumptions about gender into these systems, and asked what does it mean to put these systems in the wild and see how it plays out? Throughout all of that, I never thought of myself as a researcher.

I moved to San Francisco after my PhD to start this job in child safety. One of the big takeaways from my research was around "help-seeking"—when people in moments of duress look for help but are averse to talking to another human because they're afraid of stigma and judgment. I investigated some of the ways computer agents or nonhuman agents can play a role in facilitating that process. This was at the top of my mind when I started my role at Google as a Child Safety Product Policy Strategist. The transition to industry was not easy, but I'm glad I made it because I learned a lot about how the tech industry actually works.

I was particularly struck by the importance of knowledge production. In the child safety area, so much of the research that we use are these quantified, conservative, easily accessible forms. If you aren't an expert and rely on Google searches, then you're going to get these grifty, easy research outputs about how social media is ruining children's brains and things like that. This is garbage research in that it is not rigorous, but still, this is the research that gets encoded into the budget allocation and the product decisions that go into making these products happen. I've been shocked by this.

TK: There's an interesting phenomenon where academic researchers will kind of take on a role as a tech worker, as an Uber driver, for example. It may sound as though academic researchers are cosplaying, but having some degree of first-hand knowledge can be valuable. Do you ever find yourself wondering about your own research process now that you work at Google?

KS: When I started working at Google, I noticed all of these weird norms and practices within the tech industry. At the end of each day, I would give myself thirty minutes to do an ethnographic memo of my day, which was mostly ranting about eccentricities of being in the tech industry. But I think for folks who are ethnographically trained, you can't take that lens off. Within myself I saw a lot of tension between the mode of thinking that the industry requires of you—which is to operationalize and think about implementation—although that is a myth because we aren't implementing anything any-time soon. There is a tension between getting things done for the sake of being done with them versus the ethnographic researcher lens where you ask how these things are happening and why are they happening. Within academic spaces there can be a bit of aversion or tendency to dismiss the former, but they're different modes of inquiry and this has challenged me to be more rigorous and realistic about what it means to try to live by your principles, and at the same time, get things done with constraints on your day-to-day life.

Academics have to do this too, but the timelines and the responsibilities you have to other people are different. It's a very different way of going about doing things than the norms that we take for granted within academia where you own your work and people are more inviting, open, and generous—or, at least that's been my experience within academia.

TK: Switching back to your organizing work, how did you get involved in some of the organizing that you are doing now and what role does research play in this work?

KS: I joined the Alphabet Workers Union (AWU) when I started at Google, but after attending a few events I did not find the union inviting. It was disorganized, unclear of what was happening even while layoffs were starting to hit.

I didn't see the union stepping up in any kind of meaningful way in response to layoffs, and none could have gotten milquetoast tech workers riled up, so I decided not to get involved with the union [AWU]. It wasn't until October 7th that, at least for me, the connection between tech and what was happening in Gaza was so clear. After October 7th, along with a huge influx of tech workers, I found my way to No Tech for Apartheid.

At this point, I thought the Tech Workers Coalition was defunct, so I connected with a handful of people who seemed keen to revamp it. I was attending a bunch of meetings and trying to see where I could be most useful. The moment called for tech workers to divest and disrupt militarism in the tech industry, but we didn't have the base or the consciousness to show up in a way that's meaningful and substantively in solidarity with Palestine. Once I realized that, after the first month or so, I pivoted and focused my attention to asking, "How can we take that starting point seriously and show up in the way that's actually useful?" So, I put more energy into the Tech Workers Coalition where we were trying to build that base. I know tech workers are feeling unrepresented by their unions. The AWU didn't put out a statement about Palestine until January 2024, and that happened only after a bunch of workers put pressure on their leadership. The Communications Workers of America (CWA) also hasn't published a strong statement. Existing tech worker spaces are also uninterested in engaging with this question of internationalism. Unions remain an important ally in the organizing but it was disappointing that they couldn't show up in the moment. The existing tech groups were autonomous and disorganized. There's a culture of horizontalism in these smaller spaces that is not necessarily conducive to getting things done. Since the Tech Workers Coalition has a legacy of being effective back in 2018, and we're perceived as being a loose network of tech workers that aren't a union but more progressive than some of the other tech groups, the name can offer an inviting call for people who don't see themselves being represented by the union or other groups.

I've been helping Tech Workers Coalition develop a six-week organizing program. It's been really activating. We've had 300 people sign up from all around the world, from over seven or eight countries. Each time, we have nearly a hundred attendees. We're only on week two but we've had folks calling in at 3:00 a.m. from the UK who are hungry to learn. The resounding feedback we keep getting from participants is, "I am a tech worker, and I am so isolated. I don't know how to go about finding other people like me and starting this kind of conversation. The unions are not necessarily the right place for me." This reaffirms to me that there's a real gap. If we can show up and foster connection so that in a few months' time, we can have a disruptive impact on the militarism supply chain, I think that's what we should be heading toward. We need to do a lot of base building, relationship building, and coalition building. We can get a lot of deeply local, community-based organizing groups who have subject matter expertise and a ton of wisdom—since they have been doing this work for a long time—to come in and tell tech workers what they want or should want from other tech workers.

On the one hand, tech workers should be doing divestment calls within their workplaces, but there's a political education side of this where we need to uncover and translate how militarism actually works for members of the public. These issues are siloed and obfuscated for a reason. Tech workers also have resources and useful skills we could share with local community organizations. We did this with the San Francisco Ceasefire Resolution campaign, where we couldn't have done our messaging and communications strategy without tech support.[1] I've been grouping and coordinating around these three areas of mobilization for tech workers and trying to make clear to both community organizations and tech workers that we're building relationships.

TK: Coalition building is strategic. There's a real direct relationship between active information gathering and learning from others if the aim is being able to translate that into some kind of action.

KS: I had a funny conversation with a friend a while ago, while we worked together on writing a zine that's a guide for how you can enact solidarity, in a material way, with Palestine in this moment. We got into a heated argument about how you determine when you're moving the needle forward and how you know when you're close to a win. This friend is more of an academic. They responded with "a win is really US-centric" and "metrics are really corporate." I thought about two things in response to that. First, it's not as if people from other parts of the world have never reckoned with "how do we quantify or how do we evaluate the work that we are doing?" And secondly, that's the point of organizing. I don't know about you, but I'm here because I want to win. I want to fucking win. I want to see the contracts divested. I want to see people on the streets, and I want to win. I'm not here to have endless conversations about these big concepts when we are here in the context of organizing. We are making a commitment to translating those concepts into usable practices. If you don't want to say "win," then call it "victory" or call it whatever. I don't care about semantics; we're here to have a tangible conversation about what can actually be done.

This is something that I've often noticed with academics or scholar-activists. The scholar often comes first. That's hard to work with. You can have convoluted conversations that are not grounded in a real example. This can be off-putting to other tech workers who don't speak the same language but want to learn, and who also have important thoughts about the choice of methodology and about how we go about winning power, but don't necessarily articulate it in an academic way. At the end of the day, organizing really is about having a bunch of disagreements concerning methods. That's what we need to do. I don't want to have a conversation about semantics. I want a conversation about whether we should have an event at 10:00 a.m. or 2:00 p.m. Those are the tangible things that can sometimes be hard for folks to switch into.

TK: Are there any conversations happening about the different ways of increasing participation across the supply chain within No Tech for Apartheid? What are you observing right now within these movements?

KS: Frankly, I'm not observing much. I think this speaks to the lack of coalition, trust, and relationship building within community organizations and existing labor groups. There is a moment right now where we're able to do that, but I haven't really seen that happen in No Tech for Apartheid. That probably speaks to the perniciousness of those silos and how hard it is to organize across them. That's one of the ways research projects could really be helpful, especially with thinking about the tech-facilitated military supply chain. Being able to piece together the supply chain requires you to interact with all the different forms of labor that goes into making that happen.

To my knowledge, I don't think I've seen public-oriented educational resources able to piece that together on both the hardware side and on the software side and that's something I would like to build over the next few months. You have to reckon with the fact that there are workers who make that coordination possible at every stage of the supply chain, and that's going to require us to actually interact with different workers and understand how offices are structured, amongst other things, but I don't think we're yet at that stage to do that kind of social mapping.

TK: Jack Poulson's work has that kind of research on social mapping, combining investigative journalism and data science. He traces networks in his work at Tech Inquiry, which "maps out relationships between companies, nonprofits, and governments to better contextualize and investigate corporate influence."[2] More of that kind of work is desperately needed. It's the kind of work that Tech Workers Coalition and No Tech for Apartheid are capable of doing.

KS: That's where I get tech workers as researchers. They understand the bureaucratic side of how these things are done, so again another opportunity for tech workers to share their expertise in piecing that together. I started talking with Emily Chow from 7amleh, the Palestinian digital human rights organization. Their civil society partners are these deep community organizations with a lot of expertise but they don't know how to use social media. They don't understand how content moderation works. I proposed we have a workshop, where we have tech workers explaining end-to-end how the algorithmic content moderation works, and what are some of the practices to guard against speech suppression to increase visibility. There are definitely opportunities to learn from each other. It's not only us learning from these community organizations, tech workers have a lot to offer in terms of these skills.

I've also been trying to coordinate tech-related tasks, like running digital safety training for community members. These workshops would be geared toward people who are dealing with doxxing attacks. These harassments will likely last and escalate for a week or two but then will move on to someone else. These attacks can have lasting impacts on community members, so we need a tech worker who can sit down with them and walk them through how to disable location services on their phones. Any tech worker can quickly do that. This is another form of translation work, where having that kind of researcher mindset can be useful. Having that researcher or organizer mindset is useful where you can take a step back and look at the situation and then do a higher-level analysis to figure out what this situation is a symptom of and trying to figure out the root causes. Once we do that, we can be intentional in terms of addressing that problem. That's a skill that's often missing and needs to be cultivated in people.

MILLA VODELLO
AMAZON WORKER SOLIDARITY
In conversation with Victoria Fleming

Milla Vodello is the pseudonym of an organizer with the Amazon Worker Solidarity (AWS) group in Toronto.[1] Amazon Worker Solidarity is an independent grassroots organization of trade unionists, community activists, researchers, and workers at Amazon who recognize the fight against Amazon must be led by Amazon workers. It serves as a research and communications hub that disseminates analysis, research, and knowledge to support organizing happening on the ground at Amazon facilities in Ontario. Amazon is at the forefront of the current technological assault against workers, and since the mid-2010s, has been a core target for labor politics throughout Europe and North America.

Milla became politicized during university, where she started organizing with her campus union. Soon after graduating, she began working at an Amazon fulfillment center in the Greater Toronto Area. Milla recognizes Amazon as a key workplace for radical politics not only because of Amazon's scale and power, but because organizing Amazon workers will lead to significant changes in Canada's labor movement. She has been a labor organizer at Amazon for several years, and it is through this activity that she met Victoria Fleming.

A media and labor studies scholar from Toronto, Victoria has also been involved with Amazon workers' struggles in Canada, including through research that supported AWS' efforts to understand the company and its chokepoints.

Victoria Fleming: How did you get involved with Amazon? Why do you focus on Amazon?

Milla Vodello: The Postal Workers Union in Canada had a "salting program" for Amazon. Salting programs find people who are willing to get hired to organize a workplace. When I learned it was Amazon, I became very interested. The scope and scale of Amazon in an industry like logistics, which is important in the West, and North America in particular, could lead to a meaningful breakthrough in the labor movement. But it also requires the transformation of the labor movement to seriously take Amazon on. The story of the Amazon movement in general is that, before big unions were involved, a few socialists in different places got jobs there to organize. It's grown past that now in good and complicated ways.

VF: How do you approach organizing at Amazon as a socialist? What makes that different from other approaches?

MV: In some ways, how a socialist would approach organizing, especially at a place like Amazon, would be considered good organizing by labor movement or unionist standards. The reasons why you are doing it and what your intentions are would inform certain decisions in a different way. This approach to organizing is considered good because you're trying to develop leadership among the working class instead of focusing on mobilizing people around a specific issue who then become activated around campaigns. We're organizing to say we're contesting management for power all the time.

Even though a union, in the end, is a defensive organization, the point is to develop a parallel structure to management. Unions have their management and their interests and we should be able to have that on our side. To do that you need to be able to build up leadership in the union. You have to be systematic and specific when you're organizing so that you have the whole place organized, not just interested people who come out to things. You're constantly trying to build an organization that covers the whole of the work and the workplace. That's a very difficult task but I think it's especially necessary for Amazon.

At Amazon, we've learned—partially through our relationship with research—that the kind of strike where everyone knows about it in advance, since it happens after bargaining breaks down, won't be very effective. Stopping production is something Amazon can get around. You need to have a deep enough and wide enough organization where you can switch on and off disruption and use different disruption tactics. That will mess with them.

As an example, imagine in one facility or at a couple facilities, people slowing down work one day and working normally the next day. That would make Amazon go crazy and they wouldn't know how to deal with it. If it's a known walk out or strike, they have redundancy built into their systems so efficiently that it's easy for them to get around it. But disruption, that can be unpredictable. It needs a very high level of coordination and organization to pull off.

For organizing, people think about where the least redundant places with the smallest number of people are. They'll go there to organize because it seems to make the most sense. If you were to follow this logic, last-mile facilities would be ideal sites to organize. They're smaller, and once the package is there, if you stop it from getting somewhere, you've disrupted something. They can't reroute that same package. But we focus on the big places, what's referred to as the "first-pile facilities" [fulfillment centers, in e-commerce slang], where all the inventory first comes in that are massive and replaceable. They can reroute the work quite easily in those places. There are a few reasons why we focus on them that we think are necessary in the long term of organizing. One is for political reasons. We're in this work not only because we want to mess with Amazon. The point is to build working-class organizations. We want to go to the places where there are massive amounts of people and think about how to organize them. We need to learn how to do this in this new context. The other reason is, if we consider the disruptive approach instead of striking, fulfillment centers are good places to be. They're not easy for Amazon to move or shut down. A lot of capital is injected into these facilities as opposed to the smaller delivery facilities that can be easily shut down or moved around.

To build political power at Amazon, you have to organize the masses of workers. These masses of workers are in fulfillment centers. If you're organizing in one of these facilities it's easy to be isolated, but if you're organizing in at least two or a few it will be difficult for Amazon to isolate you. They'll feel like there's disruptive activity happening in more than one facility and it's spreading. We refer to this as a "regional strategy."

VF: What role did research play in your organizing strategies when deciding to focus on fulfillment centers rather than delivery stations?

MV: First, we had our political conclusions and knew these needed to be tested or corroborated. Research on Amazon's facilities and how Amazon functions, where they tend to put their money, what importance they place on different facilities and for what reasons, showed us that this was a good strategy beyond it being a politically relevant focus.

These fulfillment centers make up a big percentage of major industrial projects in the United States.

Additionally, Steve Maher and Scott Aquanno's recent report, "A Prime Competitor: Understanding Amazon's Market Power," analyzes how Amazon makes their money.[2] This report challenges three common arguments about Amazon that people cling to and use to assess their organizing assumptions. First, people argue that warehouses are not profitable and that Amazon Web Services makes all of Amazon's money. The second assumption is that Amazon's monopoly in the logistics sector is continuously gaining concentrated amounts of power. The third assumption is that Amazon's greatest logistical strength is that it can deliver something within a day of you ordering it, which is true and important. With these three assumptions, people focus on last-mile delivery as the site of organizing. Amazon will care the most if you stop the package from being delivered to a customer within a day. Amazon does care about this, and we're not going to pretend this doesn't matter. It does. Steve and Scott's report showed that Amazon's logistics empire is at the heart of how Amazon functions and funds its other businesses and initiatives. Amazon has a certain amount of power and capacity to deliver things that no one else does but there's still a lot of competition happening which drives them forward. They don't just have this maniacal thirst for greed, they have to consistently outpace their competition. Because of the infrastructure they've built, they're able to delay paying their suppliers right away. Their suppliers will come and sell their product on the Amazon marketplace, and Amazon uses that money as interest-free loans to continue expanding their empire by putting it into other projects through research and development.

Amazon is the industry leader in terms of spending money on research and development, and they're able to do that because of their logistics capacity. They're taking the money from third-party sellers and other vendors, expanding their operations with it, and by the time they make returns on it, they're sending it back to the supplier. It's still a high turnaround time in terms of the supplier getting their money. Importantly, Amazon's first interactions with suppliers happen at the first-pile facilities. This doesn't mean that the last mile isn't important, it means that the first pile is also important in terms of Amazon fulfilling their promises. We wouldn't know this without research.

This report is a great example of how organizers and researchers feed off each other. The researchers knew where to look and what to look at. The questions and orientations that we had gave us pertinent and important information on how to tackle Amazon but also make workers feel empowered by knowing things about their employer. Having some understanding of the complex ways Amazon works and functions is important for organizing and empowering workers.

VF: Could you talk more about this dynamic between organizers and researchers? How did this orientation toward research develop?

MV: The way people think about research, when it comes to organizing, is in a corporate campaign way. The mentality is that we need researchers to find us things for propaganda purposes or to understand who the stakeholders are. That's sometimes necessary, but there's this general idea that the organizers come up with a plan and then tell the researchers what to do. Yes, organizing can give you a particular kind of view on things and we approach research differently. Researchers also have a particular kind of skill set and view into things that organizers won't have. It's through debate and discussion as equals that we come to what is the most correct or interesting strategy. For us, our research objectives are not narrow where we're trying to figure out a handful of things. We're trying to understand Amazon in its complexity, by having guided questions that we come up with together so we can analyze the company and the initiatives surrounding it as a whole. Steve and Scott's report about how Amazon makes their money, what they care about, why and where they're expanding, and what their competitive pressures are is an example of working like this. Researchers need conversations with organizers to develop their approach, but the organizers will develop analysis and strategy through talking to researchers. It's a collaborative process of trying to come up with a shared strategy.

I think there are also two different ways people usually talk about academics in general and what their usefulness toward organizing is. There's either this tokenization of workers, where workers' lived experiences are considered the only important part of the conversation, or there's this separation between worker and researcher where academics will pontificate about random things that don't seem useful. What seems helpful, is expecting academics to come out because they want to contribute to something important, and to challenge organizers and be challenged right back. In our case, we don't have this inside-outside approach, we're political equals doing different work but trying to come to conclusions together.

VF: How did you come to this idea of research?

MV: There are many experiences in the organization that led us to this but I'll speak of my own inclination toward this approach. After witnessing dynamics with other organizing projects, where researchers and others who wanted to do real work were relegated to being a part of a solidarity committee of "supporters" who sat outside of organizing. This causes real tensions. Ideally, you want people to come and participate because they feel like it's their own project and they want to contribute to it. They're compelled in some kind of personal way to participate and help in the ways they can. If they're considered supporters who must seek direction from people, there will be tensions and questions about autonomy over work and who's directing it and why. These could be productive tensions but not if there's an inherent inequality between someone who's doing the organizing and someone who isn't.

Here, we believe that organizing is the primary thing but so do the researchers. No one has any illusions about that. When we debate, I'm not going to tell someone to shut up because they're a researcher and I'm an organizer. I think seeing that dynamic play out made me realize it's not a productive tension. It ends up wasting people's time, energy, and efforts. Our approach is that we are all a part of the organizing, making decisions together, while still understanding what is a primary and what is secondary problem and struggling over that. We want to engage in the process of struggling over our unities. If you're an external, then—whether it's a researcher, a fundraiser, a communications person—as long as you're in this thing, we're all going to have to struggle over these ideas together.

VF: You started a health and safety campaign in some warehouses. What role did research play in developing that campaign?

MV: People often think that Amazon is better on certain organizing issues, like wages or benefits, than other workplaces. Wages are not necessarily industry standard. In fact, because we're lumped in with retail and not warehousing, they're quite low. The biggest problem at Amazon, however, concern working conditions related to health and safety. If you're working too fast that means you're injuring yourself or you have repetitive strain injuries. The machinery is not necessarily properly maintained or maybe you're asked to check things improperly before you use them. Understaffing, which always happens at Amazon, ends up being a health and safety issue. Because one person is supposed to be doing at least two people's jobs, the worker ends up getting injured.

The campaigns developed around health and safety have been rooted in general research to provide a full picture of what's happening. You can do some surveying of the people you're working with, to get a sense of how people's bodies are impacted by the work. There are specific methods used and developed by researchers and organizers to survey people about health and safety in a way that becomes an organizing tool. For example, there's a method where workers come together and talk about their injuries using a body map to illustrate where it hurts. People put dots on the body map and you can see that everyone's upper backs hurt. That quickly becomes a way to talk about pain and work where you can politicize it and use it for organizing. It's also a research tool where researchers are engaged and involved in surveying people.

Getting the full health and safety picture at Amazon requires us to look at the rates of injury at warehouses in comparison to other warehouses. There's a massive discrepancy. There are many more injuries in Amazon's warehouses, despite Amazon saying they're the safest workplace to be. Amazon emphasizes health and safety quite often but they do it for liability reasons. They want to avoid liability like the plague. Health and safety issues end up happening not only because Amazon is being negligent, it's the nature of the work itself and how fast and relentless it is. I've worked in other warehouses and can attest that working at Amazon is different. It's inherently unsafe, which is why you have so many more people on accommodations and who are injured. Research helps fill out that picture.

VF: What are some of the difficulties you've faced with research? How do you translate research materials into materials for workers?

MV: I always say to researchers who approach us, let's try to find a way to make this mutually beneficial. If it's going to help your research, that's cool, but it should contribute something for us too because otherwise there is no point in us setting up a meeting with them. I don't see this situation as necessarily being malicious or anyone trying to be extractive, but I do think there needs to be reciprocity in these relationships.

The other challenge is having researchers who have useful skills that would be very helpful for us, but either they're too worried about overstepping or don't fully care about contributing to this project. It's difficult for research to be self-directed. Independent research takes time to develop.

You need time and effort to come up with proposals, plans, and ideas.

In terms of translating research materials, we have people thinking about communications and how to translate research into different forms for popular consumption. That's where our public organization, Amazon Workers Solidarity (AWS), comes in. The analysis, research, and knowledge we produce is in support of the organizing that's happening on the ground and the union building that's occurring. It's content that we put out for workers and use in our campaigns, that combines communications helping frame the campaigns, but it's also where organizers and researchers come together and talk through what's most pertinent and how to translate that to workers. Translation is a question of contextualizing more than anything else. Asking, for example, why is this information interesting?

VF: What do you see the future of labor organizing looking like? Especially at Amazon.

MV: I think there's more interest in labor organizing today. At the 2022 Labor Notes, the opening panels were about Amazon and some of the most attended panels were Amazon related.[3] With the Teamsters—the largest private sector union in North America—joining the fight against Amazon, we will see dynamic and interesting changes and challenges that I think, or at least hope, we'll learn a lot from. I do worry about the Teamsters' capacity to scale up in a good way and build the kind of working-class power that is necessary. What seems to happen is that these waves emerge which are hopeful, positive, and interesting, but they don't last. For example, with Bernie Sanders, people were very excited but then the momentum was lost and they had to go somewhere else and build something. There's this peak energy happening around Palestine organizing right now too and hopefully it will politicize a lot of people.

The question comes down to whether you're building something out of these moments or not. Building something that lasts over time is always a question and a problem. I see that potentially happening with this new uptick with labor organizing at Amazon. At the very least, with labor organizing, there's a tendency toward institutionalization there because that's what unionization is. But taking on Amazon is a very broad and adventurous thing to do and I think the future of that organizing is uncertain. I hope as it gets more complicated and more people get involved, there are some lessons learned through time that continuous generations of people who are taking this on try and understand and think through. These lessons can help people after us learn and build in different ways. I hope people continue doing the groundwork and continue building in a good sustainable way, which takes longer.

QI GE
SHENZHEN V FLEET
In conversation with Wei Ding

Qi Ge has been a taxi driver in Shenzhen, China since 2000.
He cofounded an informal WeChat-based network of grassroots fleets, known in its local form as Shenzhen V Fleet. This
worker-led cooperative network emerged in 2012, prior to
the rise of ride-hailing platforms in China. Around 2015, in
response to the growing popularity of ride-hailing platforms
such as Didi, it expanded into a national alliance involving
drivers in over a hundred cities. Qi and other drivers assem-
bled their own innovative infrastructure for ride services
by leveraging social media platforms, mobile payment apps,
bots, and other informal technologies often sourced from
gray market channels. They use social media and mobile
phones to subvert the algorithms of dominant ride-hailing
platforms, especially for pricing and job allocation. They call
the set of technologies they use an "anti-platform." Although
these grassroots fleets declined significantly during the pandemic, their worker-led organizing power and their ability to
develop bottom-up knowledge about the platform systems to
repurpose and outsmart them remain noteworthy.[1]

Wei Ding is a Professor of Communication at Shenzhen
University. She has worked with local taxi driver communi-

ties in Shenzhen for more than fifteen years to understand their technology use and daily struggles. She had this conversation as part of a collaborative project on platformization of ride-hailing in China with one of the Capacitor Collective members. As a collective, we decided to include this conversation from China to showcase some ways that workers mobilize their knowledge about digital systems and use technology to advance their interests in a nation where worker-led organizations are underdeveloped.[2] The tactics and collective strategies that are used share similarities to those in countries with established trade union systems.

Wei Ding: When did you start organizing drivers? Was Didi already around?[3]

Qi Ge: In 2012, Didi had just entered Shenzhen. Before WeChat came out, we used Weibo to communicate and we even registered on NetEase, where we published blog posts. WeChat became popular in 2012, so a dozen drivers formed a WeChat group. We had regular customers then. For example, if someone working near my neighborhood took a ride with me, I would say, "Since you often commute via taxi, why not just make it more convenient for you and for me?" I would then introduce the customer to other drivers in the WeChat group.

Although I lived in Luohu (a southern district in Shenzhen), our fleet didn't limit itself to the areas where we lived. Our plan was to have three or four fleet members in every district, working together as a unit. For example, in Luohu and in Futian, we had four or five regular fleet members; Nanshan, Bao'an, and Longgang all had fleet members. What was great about the fleet, was that when Didi came out, if I took an order from the platform but suddenly had an emergency and couldn't make it, I would arrange for one of my coworkers to replace me instead. That's how it worked.

WD: What is your background?

QG: I am a high school graduate and first came to Shenzhen as a migrant worker. I wasn't very mature back then, but I've gained more experience over these years with the WeChat fleet and have learned a lot.

WD: Back when the instant messaging service QQ was popular, didn't you think about doing something similar? Because smartphones didn't exist back then.[4]

QG: We did have QQ, but back then it was just for casual chats. The real action started with WeChat, which was much more convenient and efficient. In 2012, we were even interviewed about our fleet's model and approach to organizing by Hong Kong TV, City Discovery, and Spot News.[5]

WD: At that time, was it mainly you organizing the fleet?

QG: I was a key member. But the Shenzhen V Fleet can be described as a fleet of like-minded people—from different companies, places of origin, and household registrations—who came together to found the fleet's networks.

WD: Can you tell me how it all started?

QG: When Didi came out, we only had about a dozen people helping with the promotion of the fleet. After the promotion, we slowly formed a team, which I think happened in early 2013. At that point a guy from Qihan, Hubei Province was leading us. We were just a small group—about seven or eight drivers and not all of us were from Hubei; there were people from Henan, Northeast China, Sichuan, and all over the country. As long as you met our standard and liked our model, you were welcome. If you didn't like it, we wouldn't force you. Then, we officially founded the fleet.

WD: Did you have anyone who failed to meet the standard?

QG: In the beginning, yes, there were people who didn't follow the rules. We kicked them out, but once we did, they started causing trouble. They'd say, "Who do you think you are? You are a leader because I decide you are one. If I don't listen to you, you are nothing." We didn't take any salary at the time: it was all voluntary work, helping the fleet and working for the drivers, helping them earn money. Then we started to formalize the fleet. First, we replaced the leader.

WD: Why?

QG: I told him directly, "Are you trying to build a team or a gang?" If you want a team, a team needs rules, regulations, discipline, and organization. Back then, we only had meetings once a month. As a grassroots fleet, we essentially managed ourselves like a business. We had a tech department, a business group, and even a finance group. The only requirements for joining us was one walkie-talkie and two mobile phones. Those are the essentials. Back when we first started, we would try any new technology we thought might be useful or beneficial: fast internet speed, quick order reception, wireless Wi-Fi, solar-powered chargers, walkie-talkies. Now, the standard configuration is three or four mobile phones.

WD: When did you expand from Shenzhen to nationwide?

QG: Around 2014 or 2015. Through WeChat, we could search for people or encounter each other in person. That's how we met drivers from Guangzhou. From there, we got to know drivers in Zhuhai, who then introduced us to drivers in Shunde. Later, we realized we were all in Guangdong Province, so if I drive a passenger to Guangzhou, the WeChat fleet there would arrange an intercity return trip for me to transport passengers from Guangzhou back to Shenzhen. Sometimes, they'd arrange for us to have a meal together before heading back.

At that time, we started this Pearl River Delta alliance, which was then limited to Guangdong Province. Later, the slogan became, "We need to expand beyond the Pearl River Delta and spread nationwide." By 2015, WeChat had become a very popular and widely used platform and it was easy to find "WeFriends," as you call them. If you knew someone in Guangzhou, then you might also know someone in Hangzhou or Shanghai. If you knew someone in Shanghai, they would know someone in Harbin or Qihan, and so on. Eventually, everything just connected. That's how it became what it is today.

WD: So, it grew organically? I've heard the grassroots fleet network has expanded to dozens of cities now.

QG: Over a hundred at its peak.

WD: Tell me more about the process through which you work.

QG: In 2013 and 2014, Master Zheng (the tech person in the fleet) would handle orders by using free accelerator bots which exploited the platform system's loopholes to automatically capture high-paying orders. He would secure eight to ten lucrative orders and send them out in our WeChat group. Small orders like short-distance trips were ignored. If an order was below 80 yuan [approximately US$11], we didn't even look at it.

WD: How could Master Zheng get long-distance orders? Didi and Kuaidi (the dominant ride-hailing apps then) had just entered the market, and he already had that skill?

QG: We had technical support back then in Guangzhou . . . and now the technology is nationwide. If Guangzhou has a technology, it will spread to Shenzhen.

WD: Did the fleet in Guangzhou already have this anti-platform technology not long after Didi emerged?

QG: Indeed. They went neck to neck. But Master Zheng had access to a lot of technological resources nationwide. For example, if something came up in Guangzhou or Hangzhou in informal or gray markets, he would know about it immediately and ask if we—drivers in Shenzhen—wanted to use it. He would come to us, telling us the software costs and asking if we were interested. We weren't looking simply for subsidies. Back then, we were really thrilled that we could grab big orders by utilizing these technologies and our networks. The revenues were at least 1,000 yuan per day of work.

WD: Didn't Didi notice anything?

QG: They didn't have technical support back then, but we did. It took them a long time to plug all the loopholes.

WD: It seems like you won the first round.

QG: Once this thing came out, honestly, it was "black technology."[6] Didi and other platforms started mobilizing technical teams for defense. The entire system was loaded with a lot of software. Initially, it was simple for us. When we received orders, they would pop up in six seconds. After we installed the software, Master Zheng and other tech support at the WeChat fleet figured out how to set it so that the orders would pop up in three seconds. That gave us a three-second advantage in grabbing orders. We got the order before others even saw it, so when we succeeded in grabbing the order, they were still at three seconds in, trying to get it. Back then, technology wasn't as advanced, but since 2015, bots and accelerators evolved into automatic order-grabbing systems where we could set our preferred distance for orders. I'd set it to fifty kilometers, for instance, and wouldn't take anything under forty kilometers. Only the fifty-kilometer orders would show up. At that time, our members were constantly on the highway, going back and forth between the city and the airport. It was easy and there were a lot of benefits—no need to take all the orders, low labor intensity, and fewer violations. Those years were easy.

WD: What happened after that early phase?

QG: After establishing the WeChat fleet in Shenzhen we founded the national V Alliance. The V Alliance has branches in over one hundred cities nationwide. The Alliance's Shenzhen V fleet is just one of those branches, but we have Team Leader Yang here, the president of the entire nationwide alliance, and between eighty to 180 drivers.

WD: What was your vision at that time?

QG: One for all, all for one. People who drive are always being squeezed by Didi and other ride-hailing platforms. There's no dignity left. The last time I worked for Uber, I took an order and the customer didn't want to walk even a few meters and asked me to do a U-turn. I lost my temper and deleted the Uber app on the spot.

WD: What about the WeChat groups that are not part of Shenzhen V Fleet? Are you still sharing orders with them?

QG: Of course; if you don't share, then it's not a collective fleet. Some customers have become regulars, and if they book three or four times, they become VIPs. For example, when they have a flight, I'll suggest the best time to leave, when they'll arrive, and give them an estimate . . . and with elderly customers, sometimes I'll bring them breakfast and make all the arrangements for them. There's a sense of warmth. They trust us.

WD: But eventually the grassroots fleet experienced a networking failure?

QG: In short, the strength of V fleets in each city was not effectively utilized, the customer base was not consolidated, the internal structure was not reasonably optimized. Thus, our foundations were shaky. We were limited to a few major cities, with smaller cities watching from the sidelines, without development planning and a clear, cohesive deployment strategy. The lack of cohesion led to a situation where some people only participated if there was profit, otherwise, they would remain inactive. During the pandemic, some of the grassroots fleets collapsed and exist only in name now.

CAILEAN GALLAGHER
WORKERS' OBSERVATORY (EDINBURGH)
In conversation with Diana Limbaga and Enda Brophy

Cailean Gallagher is a historian at the University of St. Andrews and a founder of the Workers' Observatory in Edinburgh.[1] Initially supported by the Scottish Trade Union Congress (STUC), the Workers' Observatory (WO) now exists as an independent labor research initiative that assists platform and gig workers in the city with research that supports labor organizing. Inspired by the traditions of citizen data science and efforts to develop class knowledge from below within the onset of industrial capitalism, the WO is engaged in notable redevelopments of workers' inquiry for the digital economy.

Animated by academic researchers and data scientists, not only has the WO forged new applications of worker inquiry, its collaborative research endeavors have led to innovative forms of collective action and even a new labor organization (Riders Movement Edinburgh) among local gig workers. Key to the WO's activities are efforts toward the development of worker data science, through which gig workers are empowered to develop actionable knowledge on the major, on-demand, data-driven gig work platforms (e.g., Uber and Deliveroo) which algorithmically and materially shape their labor conditions. Diana Limbaga and Enda Brophy spoke with Cailean Gallagher in November of 2024 to gain some insight into the Observatory's application of digital workers' inquiry.

Diana Limbaga and Enda Brophy: Can you tell us about your background and what brought you to labor activism?

Cailean Gallagher: I became political during the 2011, post-crash political environment in Scotland and England, which initially involved organizing around universities and different kinds of movements, eventually working with the Scottish Trade Union Congress (STUC). I was always motivated to be organizing with those who didn't have space within the current labor tradition—especially precarious workers. Some of that came from my own background as a historian (which is my other hat), where I'm interested in the shifting patterns of class power, the ways in which early industrialization affected workers, and shifts that take workers from a position of relative precarity to one of potential strength.

When I started working with gig workers, I became conscious of how far outside of union thinking, structures, and mentality gig workers were. That led to a project supporting gig economy workers to explore their conditions in Glasgow and Edinburgh, and a bit of a tussle with the established unions as to the value of this. Despite that tension, I used the small resources I was allowed by the STUC to get something going, and that took the form of the Workers' Observatory. It is not linked to the STUC anymore and is its own thing.

DL and EB: How does your work as a historian inform and support your research?

CG: I'm a historian of political and economic thought. I'm interested in those who, during the "Enlightenment" period, were skeptical about claims being made about how good freedom would be for workers. There was a great trumpeting about how workers were "becoming free" in the mid-to-late eighteenth century, particularly in Scotland in the context of the massive influx of workers from the country to the cities and towns. One person in particular, Sir James Steuart, an antagonist of Adam Smith and a great inspiration to Karl Marx (*Capital* is peppered with references to his work) thought that freedom doesn't amount to much if you're tossed into a market where you're under the whim of your employer. That tradition tells me a lot about the motives of those who talk about flexibility and the opportunities for workers to go where they want to, to work as they wish, to achieve this freedom, and to be independent workers in this new, less-regulated labor paradigm. That history is important. It shows that we're not in a particularly transformed moment as a result of the rush of technologies and data and digitization, in fact, the structures are very comparable.

I'm also interested in different forms taken by workers' organizing. In Edinburgh, you had the Society of Running Stationers, called "Cadies," who were eighteenth-century gig workers in the sense that they were stationed somewhere where you would go and ask them to run an errand, and they would do it for you.[2] They wore blue flannel outfits with bags attached to them. Over the course of a century, from the 1690s to the 1780s, they organized in various forms to try and bolster their power in the city. The development of that organizational form of gig work encourages me to zoom out from the current moment, to think a bit more systematically about what the development of forms of organization takes for workers and how they can build organizations that are not going to resemble the paradigmatic twentieth-century trade unions.

DL and EB: Can you tell us more about the development of the Workers' Observatory specifically?

CG: The question is: why didn't it take the form of a classical union branch? There are various reasons. One is that unions might have felt that we were encroaching on their territory, so they wouldn't have necessarily granted space to a new model of unionizing. The other was a discussion around Edinburgh becoming a "data capital" and how work would be transformed by that. The idea was to try and push back against that by saying, "What are the experiences of the people who are supposedly being 'datafied'?" Those voices were missing and part of our initiative was to bring the perspective of workers into that city-wide discussion.

Finally, I was talking with Karen Gregory, a researcher who had been doing a lot of work around gathering workers' experiences in the city, and that led us to thinking about how to get a better initiative going, one that is based on inquiry, observing what's happening, and supporting workers to do that observational work. And, how this would give us the space to bring workers together and explore questions they had without it jumping straight into a union formation approach. It was partly about saying "workers are invisible," so how do you articulate and explore what they are in a way that contributes to how unions and the public think about gig workers?

DL and EB: In an article coauthored with Karen and Boyan Karabaliev, you discuss the relationship between workers' data science and digital workers' inquiry.[3] Can you describe these two concepts and tell us about how they connect?

CG: Digital workers' inquiry is drawing on that concept of workers' inquiry which has its genealogy, in the most classic way, in an article by Marx inviting workers to conduct investigations in the workplace. Digital workers' inquiry is trying to capture the notion that workers whose work is being affected by digital systems and technologies might investigate particular questions to help them understand their work in light of these changes.

Workers' data science is something slightly different—we derived the concept from "citizen science," that is, the involvement of citizens in research. The more radical it is, the more it gives citizens the prerogative to draw out the questions that matter and conduct things in the way that they want to. It is not about large-scale scientific processes, but rather, emphasizes well-articulated, answerable questions that make sense and have a good purpose. Workers' data science is where you're involving workers in developing projects to answer questions involving gathering, analyzing, assessing, and creating data of one form or another. Some of it is a rhetorical way to imply that "datafication" does not mean all the knowledge is held by the platforms—quite often there's a sense that platforms with masses of data have so much power that it's entirely worthless trying to push against it. We're starting to unpack the idea that whatever data you have to work with might be valuable to explore and articulate. This has led some to say, "Hang on, where's the data science in all this?" We're working with fairly small datasets and with questions that don't deploy the complex computational processes that one might associate with data science. That's a deliberate way of thinking, aimed at empowering workers to conduct investigations in the datafied economy.

DL and EB: Can you reflect on the relationship between research and labor organizing and how it has taken shape in the Workers' Observatory?

CG: First, research brings funding which can provide resources for workers to explore their conditions, meet each other, discuss their issues, and develop mutual respect for each other's skills and insights. There's something simple in bringing resources to the workers. Second, research is a way of legitimizing what workers do and say in a forum that, whether it's with policymakers or in other academic contexts, might help them get more resources and more attention. Yet it's workers who ought to figure out ways of learning and sharing knowledge, articulate what's going on, and educate one another. Third, it's extremely important that organizational forms are generated by workers. If you go in there saying, "Hey, we've got this idea for an organization," you're already framing that whole potential process as one being applied from outside. If you come in and say, "Hey, we've got some questions that we think you might have some answers to, but more importantly you might have some questions that we might all be interested in finding out the answers to," then you are framing things in a way workers might be curious about, and through that curiosity, they come to explore and explain to each other their experiences. With all the projects that we've done, there comes a critical point where workers start saying, "Not only do we now understand more, but we have the relationships, the mutual respect, and the potential to do something about it." That comes out of the research process and starts the process of collectivizing. For example, we've been bringing workers from Indian, Pakistani, and Spanish-speaking communities in the city into discussions where we work through data-mapping—a form of research that looks to understand what data is known by workers, what data is known by platforms, or what data workers would want. We use that to build a survey that they can take onto the street and gather answers about. That's obviously serving a research purpose and makes sense to workers as a project that they can get involved in from an inquiry point of view. Through that process, workers in Edinburgh generated their own identity called Riders Observatory and Organising Movement (ROOM), where they're looking to act on some of what they're learning together.

DL and EB: Can you tell us a little bit more about this movement?

CG: We were in the middle of a project based on workshops where workers sketched out this map of the data that they believed the company had, and the data that they knew they were giving the company. The choice we presented to workers was that we would see this project to the end, promoting a survey through the city, analyzing the results, and coming up with insights based on that quantitative research to answer questions they've raised. That would be the end of this research project, but the question for workers was whether to use the fact that you've come together and built these relationships to set something up in the city that will continue in whatever form you want it to take. From this common collective inquiry emerged organizing issues they felt moved to act on, for example, how certain restaurants were always making workers wait a long time for their orders or that some workers had not received their tips. So, they said, "Well, we want to set up some kind of initiative with a logo," and this way they had the fundamentals of a nascent proto union. But we were very clear that the Workers' Observatory and this initiative are two different things: agency shifts away from the researcher, so the workers can see that they have this resource at their disposal to do what they want to do. That model has worked well in the past.

DL and EB: Was this the same project where the Observatory developed a tool which can enable workers to understand their pay rates on gig platforms, or was this a different project?

CG: That was a different project for getting data from pay slips, a process that emerged out of workers' frustrations about the fact that they were given only tiny tidbits of insight into the masses of data held by the platform. Initially we explored the potential for GDPR [General Data Protection Regulation] Subject Access Requests to get the data, but instead various workers realized they could get answers by analyzing pay slips and invoices.[4] That was a fairly simple way of giving workers a tool that would reveal insights into their pay; it is also easily poolable so that we can map out changing rates over time. That project showed that tool creation can be an exciting outcome of an organizing process, and its application can be a good way of supporting workers to organize. When we ran a rates campaign in Dunfermline, we had a very simple tool to analyze pay rates for food-delivery drivers in the city, and the processing of that data was instrumental for workers to challenge falling rates and reject orders under a certain fee, because they had worked out and mapped what they thought their rates were. As we develop more tools, we'll always be thinking about that relationship where the tools are the means to an end.

DL and EB: One of the issues that tends to arise between researchers and digital workers are unequal power dynamics, which can lead to extractive relationships where academics remove knowledge from workers without offering much in return. How have you confronted these risks?

CG: One way to put it is that we've oriented our research more toward the development of methodologies than as an approach to answering questions. Our job as researchers is to think through the ways workers are engaging, discussing, and exploring things, to try and offer explanations or initiatives that might show ways that workers could do things themselves. If we're in the business of figuring out how research can be at the disposal of workers, then we need to get to a point where it is useful in terms of workers' involvement.

I don't have a background in this kind of social science, so I don't have in my mind certain frameworks or processes that are norms for conducting research into phenomena like changing labor conditions. What I do have, is a background in union organizing in precarious sectors, so when I'm thinking about developing research it's through that organizing agenda and lens. That's why, for instance, the person working on the WO project just now is not an academic researcher but is someone who works on the platform and is interested in the ways that technology is changing, without a research agenda. Collaborating is always bound to be tricky. For instance, for us academics to keep doing this work, we're going to have to publish, and for us to publish we're going to have to come into accord with the rules of the game in terms of publishing.

DL and EB: It feels like such initiatives, that are in a liminal space between the academy and labor movements, are really beginning to grapple with these issues. It'd be helpful to hear how you've thought about these questions.

CG: The motivation that underlies these projects is outside of anything academic; it's about situating yourself in the service of workers' struggle. I suppose the frank answer is, we see these risks, but our commitment to supporting workers in their struggles for freedom will ground our work and ensure that it's not diverted into other things. We take account of the fact that we're in a wider movement: some people are "salts" [organizers who join nonunion organizations with the goal of organizing them from within], some people are in the university, some people are in unions. That is the collective work identity you carry when doing this kind of research. That's difficult to sustain when your bread and butter is coming from a university and there are plenty of cases where people prioritize data gathering over workers. You need to be clear about who you are politically in this environment. If we've decided that the research is useful for advancing workers' struggles, then the onus is on us to be honest about why we're doing it, who we are, and what our convictions are outside of that professional life.

DL and EB: What are some of the main challenges the Workers' Observatory faces?

CG: Number one, in the gig economy—and with food delivery in particular—in a city like Edinburgh, you have many different communities of workers, from different parts of the world, and that composition changes all the time. In the initial stages there were quite a lot of Scots doing it, there was an influx of Spanish-speaking people pre-Brexit, then Brexit making migration from Europe more difficult led to a predominance of South Asian workers. Each of these communities tends to be integrated within itself but not necessarily with the others. Even in street-level conversations, very well-meaning people from one community can end up characterizing another community as having a particular approach to the work, which is problematic. There's this occasional narrative where people say, "People from South Asia, they will accept anything. They're just working all the time; they're doing so many hours that there's less judgment being exercised in terms of orders to accept and which to reject." It's been wonderful to see those perceptions dissolve and to see new connections between communities emerge just through the street work.

DL and EB: How have workers reacted to the Workers' Observatory, the role it plays, and the resources it offers?

CG: It's all about trust. Until trust is established, there's a great deal of natural skepticism about what on earth is going on here, and that's quite alright. It sometimes takes a while before the motives are worked out. Because it's not as if the Workers' Observatory is motiveless—it isn't, it is driven by a particular motive, which is to advance the capacity of workers to organize so that they can exert power. You have to develop a relationship, and until that time, you have to bring people along one way or another—quite often through money. In our current project, we're fortunate enough to have the funding to pay workers to participate in the workshops at a rate that is more than what they'd earn on the job. In the middle of day two of a workshop, there was still a certain degree of skepticism, but by the end we were able to explain frankly what's going on, concealing nothing about our interests and motives, what the university's got to do with it, and what our connections are with different unions. I think you get to a point where you just need to say it all as it is. Once you're honest about it, then people can make up their minds based on full disclosure, and I think that's the way skepticism is overcome.

In other cases, it's more about supporting workers to address certain questions, being interested in who they are, developing human relationships that are long-lasting and have personal dimension. It's like organizing, isn't it? You're going beyond what a researcher would ever really talk about or do, but that's because we're using research to facilitate the organizing. It's important that we train ourselves to be organizers as we do research.

DL and EB: What kinds of lessons have you learned so far?

CG: One lesson I've learned is that you shouldn't see organizing through the lens of the labor movement that you're in. Gig work looks like precarious work if you spend all your time with teachers, nurses, and administrative-level work-ers. This is not necessarily the way gig workers perceive themselves, and that's partly because you've got to see where people are coming from, quite literally. For a lot of migrants, compared to some forms of work in India, doing gig work in Edinburgh is a big step up in terms of hourly income you're making. It gives you status, and you have a degree of control over your means of production. Likewise, in Edinburgh we might regard gig work in Kolkata or Delhi as being precar-ious, but in an economy with a 40 percent informal sector it's a relatively formalized kind of work. I think I've learned a lot about inheritance of labor norms, union norms, and normative ideas of what gig work is and what fair work is that are not in accord with how workers see things. These norms are potentially going to be a really big barrier as we figure out new forms of organizing. I've learned to question the notion of precarity and to always think of the fact that migrant workers often work outside of the assumptions and customs and cultures that we associate with the labor move-ment at present.

DL and EB: What do you see on the horizon for the Workers' Observatory? What are your hopes for its future?

CG: The idea behind the Workers' Observatory is to empha-size that the character of work is quite local in the physical gig economy, and that drawing up a proper sense of what that work is like means involving the workers, wherever they are. That generates a picture of the gig economy that's going to be linked to a particular place.

I think that the exciting prospect going forward—for all those gig work contexts in different parts of the world who are experimenting with different forms of organizing—is to be able to start communicating about those differences. To do so in ways that draw out the differences, rather than the similarities, so that you see a plethora of different forms of organizing and different sets of experiences—real ways in which platformization is affecting workers. What's coming next, I hope, is a shift toward understanding that the forms organizing will take in different places will be shaped by the customs, morals, languages, rationalities, and contexts of workers in different parts of the world, as well as by the history of struggle in those places. Resituating struggles—rather than seeing gig work as a new generation of workers—is going to be important to grounding a sense of how we are in the early stages of a global movement of workers, needing to find ways to challenge the new systems of capital and the ways they extract value from labor.

EPILOGUE

When we began this collaboration in 2019, there was buzzing excitement around a wave of struggles led by workers in the digital economy, often acting autonomously from labor unions. In Canada, Italy, the United Kingdom and beyond, app workers in both food delivery and ride hailing were striking. In China, taxi drivers also took to the streets to protest the expansion of ride-hailing apps. Workers at European e-commerce facilities were mobilizing at scale for the first time ever. In the United States, there was talk of a new "tech worker movement" built around Google employees walking out to protest discrimination at the company. It was also a time of broad solidarity, in which white-collar software engineers and other office workers were connecting with gig or platform workers across the global value chain, mobilizing not only to improve conditions in their own workplaces but organizing around key issues—algorithmic wage discrimination on ride-hailing apps, the tech industry's relationship to militarism, and rampant racism and sexual harassment in tech workplace culture. That phase was not free of friction, as growing wealth inequality helped to create stark contrasts between the experiences of data annotators and white-collar office workers, or between precarious contract workers and full-time employees.

In the intervening years, major geopolitical shifts and technology hype cycles have shaped the relationship between knowledge production and digital labor movements in new directions, with new challenges and promises. The techlash of the first Trump administration gave way to the tech boom of the early pandemic. The tech crash that followed did not impact executives or shareholders, but tech's rank-and-file workers were laid off en masse and saw their job prospects dwindle. American companies once welcoming to employee resource groups and diversity, equity, and inclusion (DEI) initiatives (typically part of their own marketing and anti-union campaigns) are now closing such programs and punishing employees who speak out, while laying off workers on parental leave. Following the murder of George Floyd and the 2020 uprisings, American tech companies tolerated or co-opted organic employee movements for racial justice. Four years later, Google did not hesitate to fire fifty workers who protested against the company's involvement in the Gaza genocide, with other major tech companies adopting this approach to quell pro-Palestinian employee activism. In the meantime, the movements that shook up digital capitalism in the late 2010s have shrunk in both size and political relevance.

Now more than ever, it seems crucial for workers to have the capacity to document and archive their own organizing practices and strategies across time periods and geographies. Digital workers' inquiry provides not only an opportunity for sharing working conditions and experiences across jobs, work sites or regions, but is also a mechanism for retaining vital histories and tacit forms of knowledge that are rapidly becoming erased through layoffs or restructuring, or are lost due to the disappearance of organizing archives, such as when a social media platform goes offline or when links to web-based journalism die out. Conditions on the ground are changing quickly as companies reorganize to accommodate their investments in artificial intelligence (AI) and speculative energy infrastructures, destabilizing workplace relationships and institutional memory.

Platforms once used for political mobilization, such as Twitter and Instagram, have become openly hostile to left-leaning causes. Right-wing governments increasingly seek to own and control digital platforms, and Big Tech executives openly fantasize about replacing all workers, and maybe even users, with Artificial Intelligence. In a sense, everyone is now a precarious data worker. Bosses are using generative AI to push workers into performing work in less time and for less pay, from the video game industry to advertising.[1] Hardly anyone is safe, including software developers at major companies who are, at least in theory, soon to be replaced by Microsoft's Copilot. Artists, writers, and customer service workers are also on the frontline of these attempts at immiseration through threats of automation.

Academia is not immune either. According to tech overlords enchanted by the prospect of a university that doesn't require workers at all, academics are also at risk of being replaced by AI. In California, for example, UCLA is offering an AI-generated class built around the KUDO platform and the California State University system struck a $17 million deal with OpenAI at the same time Governor Gavin Newsom threatened to cut the system's budget by 8 percent while creating an AI Workforce Acceleration Board.[2] Even academic labor unions like the American Federation of Teachers are now partnering with AI companies like Anthropic and Open AI to, in theory, train educators on how to best incorporate AI models into their classrooms, but it is more likely that teachers will be training the AI models used to justify layoffs and increased productivity demands. Academics are feeling the squeeze along with government bureaucrats, doctors, therapists, copywriters, coders, and many other traditionally white-collar employment categories, as techno-optimists clamor to erase labor's gains through the ruse of AI's false promises of automation. As conditions on the ground change fast and casualization expands, digital workers' inquiry offers a way to document workers' experiences and develop the next organizing strategies.

We write this Epilogue from the dismal vantage point of the early months of the second Trump administration in the US, where we are facing the tech industry's blatant realignment with fascism. This is not fully unexpected or new, given Silicon Valley's right-wing roots,[3] but the prominence of Big-Tech billionaires at Trump's inauguration and Elon Musk's anti-public sector worker role in the new administration make it ever clearer. Authoritarian governments are rising globally in addition to the looming threat of new neofascist governments in Europe. Even in countries where the liberal technocratic order survives, like Canada, the far right is on the rise. Tech's reactionary trajectory, including its unhinging of its white supremacist core, can also be seen as a response to internal threats coming from the organized workers who pressured the industry to improve work conditions, sever ties with Israel and the Pentagon, and reduce contributions to climate chaos.

We are building foundations for new spaces for solidarity to emerge from the wreckage, and the peripheries of the tech industry are now the frontiers of new labor movements. Among many possible examples, the Data Labelers Association is launching in Kenya, fighting for fair pay and mental health support; Chinese truck drivers have staged multiday strikes across various cities despite the risk of political repression, pressuring the Ministry of Transport to regulate platform companies; Whole Foods workers are organizing in Philadelphia despite Amazon's attempts to block their efforts; community-based coalitions of resistance against data centers are attacking these physical embodiments of tech's growing power; movements against the forced adoption of generative AI tools—that are built on stolen labor—are blossoming, from

Hollywood actors and screenwriters striking for control over their likenesses and creative works to Indigenous-led groups like Te Hiku Media Centre pushing back against tech companies' appropriation of their languages through AI-driven translation features.[4]

As new terrains of struggle and potential for solidarities emerge, new movements spark, and many will find connections across types of work and workers. Now more than ever, in the face of growing authoritarianism and the weaponization of tech against labor, there is a need for transnational solidarity movements. As struggles circulate globally and class recomposition continues, it will be up to workers to develop and document new forms of bottom-up knowledge. This will be crucial for labor movements, but also to combat the global rise of new forms of fascism and to build a just digital future.

ENDNOTES

Preface

1 See Mostafa's conversation in this volume, pp 37.

PART 1

Notes Toward a Digital Workers' Inquiry

1 Mark Stuart, Vera Trappmann, Ioulia Bessa, Simon Joyce, Denis Neumann, and Charles Umney, "Labor Unrest and the Future of Work: Global Struggles Against Food Delivery Platforms," *Labor Studies Journal* 48, no. 3 (2023): 287–97; Hong Yu Liu, "Tech Worker Activism against Gender Discrimination in China," *Capital & Class* 47, no. 4 (2023): 511–17.

2 For instance, see Max Haiven and Alex Khasnabish, *The Radical Imagination: Social Movement Research in the Age of Austerity* (Halifax, NS and London: Fernwood/Zed Books, 2014); or Jen Gobby and Chris Dixon, "Research for Transforming the World," *Briarpatch*, March 3, 2022, briarpatchmagazine.com.

3 Dan Calacci and Alex Pentland, "Bargaining with the Black-Box: Designing and Deploying Worker-Centric Tools to Audit Algorithmic Management," *Proceedings of the ACM on Human-Computer Interaction* 6, no. CSCW2 (2022): 1–24. See also "The Data Workers' Inquiry," data-workers.org.

4 See Jamie Woodcock, "Towards a Digital Workerism: Workers' Inquiry, Methods, and Technologies," *NanoEthics* 15, no. 1 (2021): 87–98; Cailean Gallagher, Karen Gregory, and Boyan Karabaliev, "Digital Worker Inquiry and the Critical Potential of Participatory Worker Data Science for On-Demand Platform Workers," *New Technology, Work and Employment* 40, no. 1, December 19, 2023,

https://doi.org/10.1111/ntwe.12286. See also Cailean Gallagher's conversation in this volume.

5 Gigi Roggero, *Italian Operaismo: Genealogy, History, Method* (Cambridge: MIT Press, 2023).

6 See Callum Cant, *Riding for Deliveroo: Resistance in the New Economy* (London: Polity, 2019).

7 See Mario Tronti, *Workers and Capital*, trans. David Broder (London and New York: Verso, 2019). Tronti's book, *Operai e capitale*, was originally published in 1966 by Einaudi Editore.

8 See notesfrombelow.org. For contemporary inquiries, including with sex workers and interns, see the work of the francophone literary journal *Ouvrage* in Montreal.

9 On composition and recomposition in digital capitalism, see Nick Dyer-Witheford, *Cyber-Proletariat: Global Labour in the Digital Vortex* (London: Pluto Press, 2015). For an example of recomposition across workers and the broader communities they are enmeshed with, see Valentina Castellini, "Spaces of social recomposition: resisting meaningful work in social cooperatives in Italy," *Antipode* 53, no. 6 (2021): 1661–81.

10 For instance, Microsoft Research provides fellowships and research funding to scholars through its Social Media Collective and Microsoft Research AI & Society fellows program; major research conferences such as FAccT (the Conference on Fairness, Accountability, and Transparency) and research organizations such as PAI (the Partnership on AI think tank) are funded by companies including Adobe, Meta, Google, and Amazon.

11 Ifeoma Ajunwa, Sareeta Amrute, Lilly Irani, Winifred R. Poster, and Meg Stalcup, "Tech firms need Black AI scholars and labour rights," *Nature* 590, no. 389 (2021), https://doi.org/10.1038/d41586-021-00407-2.

12 Meredith Whittaker, "The Steep Cost of Capture," *Interactions* 28, no. 6 (2021): 50–5.

13 Patricia Hill Collins, "Learning from the outsider within: The sociological significance of Black feminist thought," *Social Problems* 33, no. 6 (1986): s14–s32; on co-research, see Gigi Roggero, "Notes on Framing and Re-inventing Co-research," *ephemera* 14, no. 3 (2015): 515–23.

14 Nina B. Wallerstein and Bonnie Duran, "Using Community-based Participatory Research to Address Health Disparities, *Health Promotion Practice* 7, no. 3 (2006): 312–23.

15 Antonio Gramsci, *Selections from the Prison Notebooks*, trans. Quintin Hoare and Geoffrey Nowell Smith (New York: International Publishers,1971): 323–46.

16 Feminist criticism of the situated knowledge production regime resonates with postcolonial approach toward studies of science and technology. Both are powerful in revealing the limitations of positionality. See Donna Haraway, "Situated Knowledges: The Science Question in Feminism and the Privilege of Partial Perspective," *Feminist Studies* 14, no. 3 (1988): 575–99; or Sandra Harding, "Postcolonial and Feminist Philosophies of Science and Technology: Convergences and Dissonances," *Postcolonial Studies* 12, no. 4 (2009): 401–21.

17 For more on research methods incorporating workers' tacit knowledge into analysis, see Callum Cant, Clark McAllister, Zeynep Karlıdağ, George Briley, and Dante Philp, "Workers' Inquiry: A User's Guide," in *SAGE Handbook of Digital Labour*, ed. Ergin Bulut, Julie Chen, Rafael Grohmann, and Kylie Jarrett (London et al.: SAGE Publications Ltd., forthcoming 2025).

18 For a firsthand account, see Tech Workers Coalition, "Tech Workers, Platform Workers, and Workers' Inquiry," *Notes from Below* 2, March 30, 2018, notesfrombelow.org.

19 Facility Waters and Jamie Woodcock, "Far from Seamless: A Workers' Inquiry at Deliveroo," *Viewpoint Magazine*, September 20, 2017, viewpointmag.com.

20 DAIR's Data Workers' Inquiry, data-workers.org.

21 Workers' Observatory in Edinburgh, workersobservatory.org.

22 Tamara Kneese, "Precarity Beyond the Gig: From University Halls to Tech Campuses," in *The Gig Economy: Workers and Media in the Age of Convergence*, ed. Brian Dolber, Michelle Rodino-Colocino, Chenjerai Kumaniyka, and Todd Wolfson (London and New York: Routledge, 2021): 239–55.

23 Nick Srnicek, *Platform Capitalism* (London: Polity, 2015).

24 Andrea Zeffiro, "Digitizing Labor in the Google Books Project: Gloved Fingertips and Severed Hands," in *Humans at Work in the*

Digital Age: Forms of Digital Textual Labor, ed. Shawna Ross and Andrew Pilsch (London and New York: Routledge, 2019), 133–53.

25 Lilly Irani, "Turkopticon as Software, Turkopticon as Worker Organizing: On Organizing Form as Emergent Strategy (2009–2024)," in *SAGE Handbook of Digital Labour*, ed. Ergin Bulut, Julie Chen, Rafael Grohmann, and Kylie Jarrett (London et al.: SAGE Publications Ltd., forthcoming 2025).

26 Karen Gregory, "'Worker Data Science' Can Teach Us How to Fix the Gig Economy," *Wired*, December 7, 2021, wired.com.

27 Lilly Irani, "Justice for Data Janitors," *Public Books*, January 15, 2015, public-books.org.

28 The *Bits in the Machine* zine can be downloaded at collective action.tech.

29 Paul Christopher Gray, "The Same Tools Work Everywhere: Organizing Gig Workers with Foodsters United," *Labour/Le Travail* 90, no. 1 (2022): 41–84.

30 This project was completed thanks to the research work of Véronique Sioufi, a PhD student in the Department of Geography at Simon Fraser University.

31 Alphabet Workers Union, "Every Google Worker: An Examination of Alphabet's US Shadow Workforce," c. 2019, https://everygoogleworker.alphabetworkersunion.org.

32 Wei Ding, "Platform Poachers: Media Tactics and the Spatial Production of Civilian Fleets in Shenzhen," *Chinese Journal of Journalism & Communication*, no. 6 (2023): 6–32. [In Chinese.]

33 On information asymmetry at Uber, see Alex Rosenblat and Luke Stark, "Algorithmic Labor and Information Asymmetries: A Case Study of Uber's Drivers," *International Journal of Communication* 10 (2016): 3758–84; on calculative logics, see Aaron Shapiro, "Dynamic Exploits: Calculative Asymmetries in the On-demand Economy," *New Technology, Work and Employment* 35, no. 2 (2020): 162–77; the concept of epistemic injustice is developed in Chi Kwok, "Epistemic Injustice in Workplace Hierarchies: Power, Knowledge and Status," *Philosophy & Social Criticism* 47, no. 9 (2021): 1104–31.

34 See Jenna Burrell, "How the Machine 'Thinks': Understanding Opacity in Machine Learning Algorithms," *Big Data & Society* 3, no. 1 (2016); Rob Kitchin, "Thinking Critically About and Researching

Algorithms," in *The Social Power of Algorithms*, ed. David Beer, 14–29 (Abingdon, Oxon and New York: Routledge, 2018).

35 Waters and Woodcock, "Far from Seamless."

36 See Arianna Tassinari and Vincenzo Maccarone, "Riders on the Storm: Workplace Solidarity among Gig Economy Couriers in Italy and the UK," *Work, Employment and Society* 34, no. 1 (2020): 35–54; Daniela Leonardi, Marco Briziarelli, Emiliana Armano, and Annalisa Murgia, "The Ambivalence of Logistical Connectivity: A Co-research with Foodora Riders," *Work Organisation, Labour & Globalisation* 13, no. 1 (2019): 155–71.

37 For an example of workers reverse engineering a food delivery app in Berlin, see Niels Van Doorn, "At What Price? Labour Politics and Calculative Power Struggles in On-demand Food Delivery," *Work Organisation, Labour & Globalisation* 14, no. 1 (2020): 136–49.

38 RideFair Coalition, "Legislated Poverty," ridefair.ca.

39 For an early theorization of these dynamics, see Raniero Panzieri, "Sull'uso delle macchine nel neo-capitalismo," *Quaderni Rossi* 1 (1961). An English translation can be found at libcom.org.

40 On Chinese delivery work, see Ya-Wen Lei, "Delivering Solidarity: Platform Architecture and Collective Contention in China's Platform Economy," *American Sociological Review* 86, no. 2 (2021): 279–309. On Chinese data workers, see Tongyu Wu and Bingqing Xia, "Computing and Manipulating: The Complementary Organization to Algorithms in the Data Labeling Work," *Sociological Review of China* 11, no. 6 (November 20, 2023): 66–86. [In Chinese.] On augmented despotism at Amazon, see Alessandro Delfanti, *The Warehouse: Workers and Robots at Amazon* (London: Pluto Press, 2021).

41 For more, see Lilly Irani and M. Six Silberman, "Turkopticon: Interrupting Worker Invisibility in Amazon Mechanical Turk," in *Proceedings of the SIGCHI Conference on Human Factors in Computing Systems*, 2013, 611–20; Enda Brophy and Seamus Bright Grayer, "Platform Organizing: Tech Worker Mobilization and Digital Tools for Labour Movements," in *The Gig Economy: Workers and Media in the Age of Convergence*, ed. Todd Wolfson, Chenjerai Kumanyika, Michelle Rodino-Colocino, and Brian Dolber (London and New York: Routledge, 2021), 207–22.

42　David Moscrop, "Organizing a Union? Yes, There's an App for That," *Jacobin*, January 30, 2023, jacobin.com.

43　For more on RDU's organizing, see Brian Dolber, "Organizing at the Digital Water Cooler: Social Media, Platform Organizing, and the Fight Against Surveillance Capitalism," *South Atlantic Quarterly* 122, no. 4 (2023): 779–93.

44　For examples of algorithmic sabotage and resistance, see Tiziano Bonini and Emiliano Treré, *Algorithms of Resistance: The Everyday Fight against Platform Power* (Cambridge, MA and London: The MIT Press, 2024). On e-commerce in Italy, see Delfanti, *The Warehouse*; on ride-hailing in China, see Julie Yujie Chen, "Thrown under the bus and outrunning it! The logic of DiDi and taxi drivers' labour and activism in the on-demand economy," *New Media & Society* 20, no. 8 (2018): 2691–711.

45　On these mobilizations, see Cant, *Riding for Deliveroo*; Bonini and Treré, *Algorithms of Resistance*.

46　See Dolber, "Organizing at the Digital Water Cooler"; Katie J Wells, Kafui Attoh, and Declan Cullen, "'Just-in-Place' Labor: Driver Organizing in the Uber Workplace," *Environment and Planning A: Economy and Space* 53, no. 2 (March 1, 2021): 315–31.

47　Tamara Kneese, "Our Silicon Valley, Ourselves," *b2o*, August 6, 2021, boundary2.org.

48　Seamus Bright Grayer and Enda Brophy, "The Party's Over: Organizing Across the Contractor Divide at Google," in *The Handbook of Digital Labor*, ed. Jack Qiu, Richard Maxwell, and Shinjoung Yeo (London and New York: Wiley Blackwell, 2025), 18–37.

49　Formed in the United States in 1975, the Zerowork Collective was a transatlantic group of militant scholars who, through two issues of an eponymous journal, aimed to explore the working class "defined by its struggle against capital." See Zerowork, "Introduction" (1975), zerowork.org.

50　"Unions are inherently contradictory," writes British labor organizer Ian Allinson. "They are organisations of resistance to employers, but we also use unions to agree to the terms of our exploitation with management." Ian Allinson, *Workers Can Win* (London: Pluto Press, 2022), 210.

51 Jane McAlevey, *No Shortcuts: Organizing for Power in the New Gilded Age* (Oxford and New York: Oxford University Press, 2016). See also Veena Dubal, "Sectoral Bargaining Reforms: Proceed with Caution," in *New Labor Forum*, January 20, 2022, newlaborforum. cuny.edu.

52 The International Association of Machinists formed, effectively, a company union with Uber in New York. Similar agreements have been reached with United Food and Commercial Workers Canada, the GMB Union in the UK, and the Transport Workers Union in Australia.

53 For a discussion of the potential pitfalls of researcher protagonism vis-à-vis power imbalances with workers, see Todd Wolfson, Ursula Huws, James Farrar, and Yaseen Aslam, "'Alongside but Not in Front': Reflections on Engagement, Disengagement and Ethics in Action Research with Workers," *Work Organisation, Labour & Globalisation* 16, no. 1 (2022): 104–20.

54 The stories and a free ebook are available at afteramazon.world.

PART 2

Mostafa Henaway
Immigrant Workers Centre (Montreal)

1 Mostafa Henaway, "Infiltrating Amazon," *The Breach*, November 11, 2021, breachmedia.ca; Mostafa Henaway, *Essential Work, Disposable Workers: Migration, Capitalism and Class* (Halifax: Fernwood, 2023).

2 For more about this historic campaign of the Toronto Coalition of Concerned Taxi Drivers, see Mostafa's conversation with Ahmet Gulkan, conducted with Stefan Christoff, "Taxi Cabs and Capitalism in Toronto!!," *LeftTurn*, November 1, 2005, leftturn.org. After more than thirty years of radical, anticapitalist organizing, Ontario Coalition Against Poverty (OCAP) ceased operations in 2023.

3 The Temporary Foreign Worker Program (TFWP) allows Canadian employers to hire foreign nationals to fill labor shortages in Canada but does not provide a clear path to permanent residence or citizenship.

4 In February 2025, Amazon shut down all its Quebec warehouses, putting thousands of employees out of work just a few months after a successful unionization drive in Laval.

5 Henaway, "Infiltrating Amazon."

Alex Hanna
Distributed AI Research Institute

1 Alex Hanna, "On Racialized Tech Organizations and Complaint: A Goodbye to Google," *Medium*, February 2, 2022, alex-hanna. medium.com.

2 Giulio Regeni, an Italian PhD student at the University of Cambridge, was kidnapped in Cairo in 2016 while researching local labor unions. He was found dead, with signs of having been tortured, near an Egyptian secret service prison. The military regime never collaborated with Italy to provide the details of Regeni's death.

3 TGIF (Thank God it's Friday) sessions were "all-hands" meetings, in which employees could ask questions to Google's management.

4 Project Maven is a Pentagon initiative to use machine learning to process data that informs weapon systems. As a result of Google worker organizing, the company withdrew from the project in 2018.

5 Meredith Whittaker, the current CEO of Signal, was the founder of Google's Open Research Group and a cofounder of AI Now Institute. Amr Gaber is a software engineer and organizer with the Tech Workers Coalition.

6 Cher Scarlett and Janneke Parrish are cofounders of the #Apple-Too movement, which aimed to expose discrimination, harassment, and pay disparities as systemic labor issues at Apple. The movement encouraged employees to share their experiences at the company, leading to nearly 500 reports from workers within the first few weeks which the organization posted online.

7 The CWA is the largest communications and media labor union in North America. The Alphabet Workers Union (AWU), established in January 2021, represents workers across Alphabet, including contractors at Google. Affiliated with the CWA as Local 9009, AWU functions as a "solidarity" or "wall-to-wall" union, encom-

passing full-time employees, contractors, and temporary workers without seeking formal collective bargaining rights through the National Labor Relations Board (NLRB).

Krystal K and Phil
Turkopticon

1 "Human Intelligence Tasks" (HITs) is what Amazon Mechanical Turk calls the tasks it outsources·to its workers.

2 Krystal Kauffman and Adrienne Williams, "Turk Wars: How AI Threatens the Workers Who Fuel It," *Stanford Social Innovation Review*, October 11, 2023, ssir.org.

Tyler Sandness
Rideshare Drivers United

1 Eliza McCullough, Brian Dolber, Justin Scoggins, Edward-Michael Muña, and Sarah Treuhaft, "Prop 22 Depresses Wages and Deepens Inequities for California Workers," National Equity Atlas, September 21, 2022, nationalequityatlas.org.

Mikaiil Hussein and Peter Zschiesche
United Taxi Workers of San Diego

1 Erik Olin Wright, *How to Be an Anti-Capitalist in the 21st Century* (London and New York: Verso, 2019). Additional motivation for this project can be found in Udayan Tandon, Lilly Irani, Peter Zschiesche, and Mikaiil Hussein, "About United Taxi Cooperative," *Verso Own This! Roundtable*, January 31, 2024, versobooks.com.

2 Jill Esbenshade et al., "Driven to Despair: A Survey of San Diego Taxi Drivers," May 2013, San Diego State University and the Center on Policy Initiatives, ccre.sdsu.edu.

3 For one account of these barriers, see Udayan Tandon, Vera Khovanskaya, Enrique Arcilla, Mikaiil Haji Hussein, Peter Zschiesche, and Lilly Irani, "Hostile Ecologies: Navigating the Barriers to Community-Led Innovation," *Proceedings of the ACM on Human-Computer Interaction*, Volume 6, Issue CSCW2 (2022): 1–26, https://doi.org/10.1145/3555544.

RK Upadhya
Tech Workers Coalition (Bay Area)

1 Log Out! Worker Resistance in the Platform Economy, University of Toronto, McLuhan Centre for Culture and Technology, March 6, 2018.

2 UNITE HERE is a labor union for 300,000 workers in the hotel, gaming, food service, manufacturing, textile, distribution, laundry, transportation, and airport industries in the US and Canada. For more information see unitehere.org.

3 Conjunctural analysis is a tool, rooted in a history of Marxist analysis and political and social movements, for the mapping of social forces to make a political intervention.

Erik H
Tech Workers Coalition (Seattle)

1 "Abolitionist Cybernetics: Groceries from South Bay Mutual Aid," *Tech Workers Coalition Newsletter*, January 25, 2022, techworkerscoalition.org.

2 The union ended up organizing a walkout for the 2025–2027 contract negotiations, before the students returned in fall 2025. Erik and fellow food service workers were allowed to join it with management approval. A video of the walkout can be found on YouTube, https://youtu.be.

Kate Sim
No Tech for Apartheid

1 A grassroots campaign that, in January 2024, pushed the City and County of San Francisco to adopt a resolution calling for a sustained ceasefire in Gaza.

2 See Tech Inquiry, techinquiry.org.

Milla Vodello
Amazon Worker Solidarity

1 AWS is also the acronym of Amazon Web Services, the cloud computing platform owned and operated by Amazon.

2 Stephen Maher and Scott Aquanno, "A Prime Competitor: Understanding Amazon's Market Power," Amazon Worker Solidarity, October 9, 2024, amazonworkersolidarity.ca.

3 Labor Notes is a conference by and for rank-and-file unionists and labor activists from the US, Canada, and Mexico. It takes in place in Chicago every two years. See labornotes.org.

Qi Ge,
Shenzhen V Fleet

1 We are grateful for Wei Ding's generosity in sharing this conversation and giving us permission to include this English translation in the book.

2 China has state-sanctioned trade unions called All China Federation of Trade Unions, but they are not led or governed by workers.

3 Known as Didi Dache when it launched in 2012, Didi merged with and acquired competitors around 2015–2016, expanding to become China's largest and most popular ride-hailing system, and now, DiDi Global.

4 QQ is an instant messaging service developed by Chinese company Tencent, initially released in 1999.

5 The latter two are local TV channels in Shenzhen.

6 If your technology is described as "black" [hei] in China, it typically means that it is advanced technology or related to hacking. Qi is referring to the use of low-cost digital tools (e.g., bots) to maneuver the operation of platform algorithms, so here, black technology is comparable to a grassroots hack.

Cailean Gallagher
Workers' Observatory (Edinburgh)

1 For more information, see workersobservatory.org.

2 Cailean Gallagher and Jeremy Knox, "Cadies, Clocks and the Data-driven Capital: Incorporating Gig Workers in Edinburgh," in *Data Justice and the Right to the City*, ed. Morgan Currie (Edinburgh: Edinburgh University Press, 2022), 190–210.

3 Cailean Gallagher, Karen Gregory, and Boyan Karabaliev, "Digital Worker Inquiry and the Critical Potential of Participatory Worker Data Science for On-Demand Platform Workers," *New Technology, Work and Employment* 40, no. 5, December 19, 2023, https://doi.org/10.1111/ntwe.12286.

4 A General Data Protection Regulation Subject Access Request enables individuals in the European Union (and the UK, under equivalent laws) to obtain detailed information about how their personal data is being used by an organization.

Epilogue

1 For interviews with workers affected by AI, see Brian Merchant, "AI Is Already Taking Jobs in the Video Game Industry," *Wired*, July 23, 2024, wired.com.

2 A California State University (CSU) press release documents the State Governor's budget stick-and-AI carrot: "CSU Announces Landmark Initiative to Become Nation's First and Largest AI-Empowered University System," February 4, 2025, calstate.edu/csu-system/news/Pages/CSU-AI-Powered-Initiative.aspx.

3 Becca Lewis, "'Headed for Technofascism': The Rightwing Roots of Silicon Valley," *The Guardian*, January 29, 2025, theguardian.com; David Golumbia, *Cyberlibertarians* (Minneapolis: University of Minnesota Press, 2024).

4 For more information, see Te Hiku Media, tehiku.nz.

CONTRIBUTORS

Enda Brophy is a professor at Simon Fraser University in Vancouver.

Julie Yujie Chen is an assistant professor at the University of Toronto.

Hiu Fung Chung is a PhD candidate at the University of Toronto.

Alessandro Delfanti is a professor at the University of Toronto.

Wei Ding is a professor at Shenzhen University.

Brian Dolber is an associate professor at California State University San Marcos.

Catherine Dubé is a graduate of the Simon Fraser University School of Communication.

Victoria Fleming is a PhD candidate at York University in Toronto.

Cailean Gallagher is an associate lecturer at the University of St. Andrews.

Qi Ge is a taxi driver with the Shenzhen V Fleet.

Seamus Bright Grayer is a graduate of the Simon Fraser University School of Communication.

Erik H is an organizer, systems engineer, and food service worker in Seattle.

Alex Hanna is director of research at the Distributed AI Research Institute.

Mostafa Henaway is an organizer with the Immigrant Workers Centre in Montreal.

Mikaiil Hussein is the President of United Taxi Workers of San Diego.

Lilly Irani is a professor at the University of California San Diego.

Krystal K and **Phil** are organizers at Turkopticon.

Tamara Kneese is a research director at Data & Society Research Institute.

Diana Limbaga is a graduate student at Simon Fraser University.

Sarah Jean Salman is a PhD student at Cornell University.

Tyler Sandness is a member of Rideshare Drivers United and former Lyft driver.

Kate Sim is a researcher and organizer with No Tech for Apartheid and Tech Workers Coalition.

Véronique Sioufi has a PhD in Labour Geography and is the Racial and Socio-Economic Equity policy analyst at the progressive think tank BC Society for Policy Solutions.

RK Upadhya is an electrical engineer based in San Antonio and an organizer with Tech Workers Coalition and Industrial Workers of the World.

Milla Vodello is the pseudonym of an organizer with the Amazon Worker Solidarity group in Toronto.

Peter Zschiesche is a founder of the Employee Rights Center in San Diego.

ABOUT COMMON NOTIONS

Common Notions is a publishing house and programming platform that fosters new formulations of living autonomy. We aim to circulate timely reflections, clear critiques, and inspiring strategies that amplify movements for social justice.

Our publications trace a constellation of critical and visionary meditations on the organization of freedom. By any media necessary, we seek to nourish the imagination and generalize common notions about the creation of other worlds beyond state and capital. Inspired by various traditions of autonomism and liberation—in the US and internationally, historical and emerging from contemporary movements—our publications provide resources for a collective reading of struggles past, present, and to come.

Common Notions regularly collaborates with political collectives, militant authors, radical presses, and maverick designers around the world. Our political and aesthetic pursuits are dreamed and realized with Antumbra Designs.

www.commonnotions.org
info@commonnotions.org